LIZARD TALES
The Wit & Wisdom of Ron Shirley

Ron Shirley

THREE RIVERS PRESS · NEW YORK

Published in the United States by Three Rivers Press, an imprint of the
Crown Publishing Group, a division of Random House, Inc., New York.
www.threeriverspress.com
www.crownpublishing.com

Three Rivers Press and the Tugboat design are registered
trademarks of Random House, Inc.

Originally published in paperback in the United States in different
form by EME Press, East Stroudsburg, PA, in 2010.

The photos appearing herein are courtesy and property of the author.

Library of Congress Cataloging-in-Publication Data
Shirley, Ron.
Lizard tales / Ron Shirley.
p. cm.
1. Shirley, Ron. 2. Collection agents—North Carolina—Lizard Lick—
Biography. 3. Conduct of life. 4. Lizard Lick (N.C.)—Social
life and customs. I. Title.
HD8039.C6462U674 2012
658.8'8—dc23   2012024541

ISBN 978-0-385-34726-6
eISBN 978-0-385-34727-3

Printed in the United States of America

Book design by Lauren Dong
Cover design by Steve Attardo

10 9 8 7 6 5 4 3 2 1

First Three Rivers Press Paperback Edition

*This book is dedicated to my wife, Amy,
and my mother, Judy.
They both taught me that love isn't love
until you give it away, and that letting go is
the greatest way to hold on.*

Contents

Ronisms

10 Ronisms

Introduction

I'm an adrenaline junkie. For me, life just ain't no fun if it's not fast and furious and full of surprises.

I was a college football player when one day I got struck by lightning and fell off a roof. After a couple weeks in the hospital, I got out to discover that football was gone for me . . . and with it, my plans for the future. I really didn't know what to do. I tried working in the office of my brother's car lot for a while, but I'm just not the kind of guy who can sit behind a desk; it left me as antsy as a bee-stung stallion—that is, until my brother started doin' his own financing and I started repoing cars for him. I never would've guessed that was gonna be the start of a whole new life for me, ultimately as founder and president of Lizard Lick Towing and Recovery—a life that is many things, but never, ever boring! What follows in these pages is a collection of true stories from this always-unpredictable life of mine.

I'm a person who craves mental challenges as much as physical ones. Now, you might not think that the repo business requires a lot of smarts, but I'll tell you what: it's all a mental chess game. I find ways to find people, and for me that's the fun of this business. Of course, the actual finding isn't always fun—I've been stabbed, I've had guns pulled on me . . . you can read about all that in the pages ahead. I gotta say, though, in this process I sure have learned a whole lot. That's where the "wisdom" part of this book comes from—many a life lesson learned the hard way.

And the funny way. In this business, anybody can be tough. I found a way to separate myself from the rest of the pack by using funny sayings to put people off guard and take control of the situation—maybe letting me get the job done with wit rather than force . . . and hopefully living to tell about it! When I'm out there repoing a man's truck and he's about to bust my head open like a gourd, I might say, "Bo, you look as crazy as a three-eyed dog in a hubcap factory."

And he loses it! He doesn't know what to say or what to think—and then I'm in control.

These little secret weapons of mine are what have come to be known as Ronisms. Now, the truth be told, they're not all mine. My granddaddy used to say some of these things. And my momma used to say some of these things.

Some of these sayings have been around for more than a hundred years—those are the ones I learned growin' up in the cut, and over time I've tried to perfect 'em and make 'em my own. Others are truly original. But original or not, these Ronisms have become something of my trademark, and now they're part of my everyday life. So, naturally, they're part of all these stories from my life. In between the stories, you'll find a whole bunch more sayings. Try 'em out yourself . . . and feel free to adapt 'em and change 'em and make 'em your own—just like I did.

So that's what this book is: funny sayings and hard-learned lessons from the life of a man on a constant quest for the next adventure. Or, in other words, *The Wit & Wisdom of Ron Shirley.*

I've heard it said that a man is a success if he gets up in the morning and gets to bed at night, and in between he does what he wants to do. Well, if that's true, then I'm proud to be a successful man. And if telling you about it can make you laugh a little, and maybe even learn a little, then I'll be happier than a raccoon in the corn crib with the dogs tied up to have helped a bit with your success. So kick back, put your feet up, help yourself to some 'shine (if you got it), and enjoy these true stories about the guy they call the Big Lizard—or what I like to call *Lizard Tales.* Now turn the page and GET LICKED!

1

This Is a Dog-Eat-Dog World . . . So Don't Come Around Wearin' No Milk-Bone Underwear

Momma always told me that if you eat one live toad first thing in the morning when you wake, nothing worse will happen to you the rest of the day. I think she was right.

One Saturday morning, me and Jason woke up just before daylight, and it didn't take us more than fifteen minutes to be bored and looking for something mischievous to get into. Now, many of you have met boys like me and Jason before—but you probably had to pay admission. See, we've always been of the understanding that you shouldn't take life too seriously. Heck, no one gets out alive anyway. So we ventured outside to the shed to see what we could develop or destroy.

Now, Jason never was the brightest crayon in the box. I remember one time he took an IQ test and the results came back negative. But that boy was sure gifted with his hands. He could build or fly most anything I could think up, so I decided, since he was so useful, I'd keep him around. Well, we went to rumbling and somehow ended up with some bottle rockets, an old stuffed toy dog, and a pair of broken roller skates. Jason was talking about making some bottle rocket–propelled skates, but I was more interested in making a skate-propelled dog. I figured we could put some wheels on the mutt, strap the rockets to his hindquarters, get up in the curve on the road, and shoot him across when a car was coming around the bend.

Jason said we'd have a better chance of freezing moonshine in a woodstove than pulling this off without Momma or Pops catching us. But I could sell ketchup to a tomato farmer. And I knew Jason.

"You'd rather drink five gallons of gas and then piss on a forest fire than not go along," I told him. He quickly agreed and we went to work.

For about two hours, we were busier than a stump full of termites in a flash flood. Then, when Jason attached the last bottle rocket, I knew even Einstein would have been impressed. So we grabbed our new invention, hopped on our bicycles, and headed down the road. We hid the bikes in the tree line and set up our new four-legged friend, whom we named Run Over Rover. Then we waited for our first victim.

Just as we saw a big blue Pontiac top the hill, I lit the fuses and eased Rover to the white line. About the time the car entered the curve, ol' Rover launched right out in front of it. We heard the brakes lock up. White smoke went rolling. And that car turned sideways right there in the middle of that curve.

Jason was as nervous as a pit bull crapping thumbtacks on a balloon ride, but I was rolling in the ditch laughing like a clown on crack—until I heard the car door slam. I looked up and standing over me was one of the biggest women I'd ever seen. It wasn't just the fact that she looked mean enough to scare the balls off a low-flying duck; you could tell she was wound up tighter than a minister's wife's girdle at an all-you-can-eat pancake breakfast. She started in on me and Jason about how we could have got that poor dog killed by running him out in the road like that, not to mention that someone could damage their car trying to avoid him. I ran over, picked up Rover, and said, "Calm down, lady. He ain't even real—see?" And I showed her the fake dog and the wheels, thinking this would calm her down a little. But I could see the fire light up in her eyes and could tell she was getting ready to slap me so hard that when I woke up my clothes would be back in style. So I did what any self-respecting older brother would do: I blamed it on Jason . . . 'cause I knew he could run faster!

"Lady, I was just out here watching! That guy built it and brought it out here." As soon as she turned to Jason, I became as scarce as hens' teeth. Poor ol' Jason was pinned down by that woman, stuck there like a bumblebee in a bucket of tar.

Now, apart from not being too bright, Jason was also known to have a mouth big enough to stick a hook in. As I ran by, I heard him yelling, "Lady, if I wanted to hear from a butthole, I'd fart!"

Before I knew it he was passing me, running across that field. And when we got to the tree line we stopped, looked back, and saw that lady standing in that curve waving her arms at us and looking meaner than a skillet full of snakes. We couldn't make out much of what she was saying; but after all the hand gestures, I am pretty sure she figured me and Jason were the reason God gave people their middle finger.

We spent the next few hours lighting bottle rockets, watching cars slide off the road, and running into the woods. We were having more fun than a Texas tornado in a trailer park, but we were getting low on propulsion fuel and needed breakfast, so we figured we would get us one more and call it a day.

As a black truck topped the hill, Jason lit Rover and we got ready to run. About the time the truck hit the curve and Rover hit the line, we had already started laughing, just waiting for the brakes to lock and the white smoke to roll. Instead, I heard that truck motor rev up and kick into passing gear. The driver had floored that mug and was swerving directly toward Rover. Next thing I know, Rover had taken flight and exploded on impact. Pieces of him were flying everywhere. Me and Jason just looked at each other in disbelief, not even realizing the truck had stopped until I heard both doors slam. Right then my rear drew up tighter than a mosquito's butt in a nosedive, and I looked up to see the same lady from earlier in the day. Only this time, she had brought her husband back—and he wasn't none too happy.

This ol' boy looked like he got left in the outhouse when lightning had struck. He reached down and yanked us both up by our earlobes. I don't know what he was madder about: running over Rover in front of his wife, or the way Jason had spoken to her that morning. But I knew we had to get out of there before he took us to Momma and Pops, and it appeared that was gonna be harder than herding heartless chickens.

Well, he was holding us, and the lady was scolding us like sinners at a prayer meeting, when I noticed Jason sliding the rest of the bottle rockets into the back pocket of that man's overalls. I looked up at the man and told him, "You'd rather shove a wet noodle up a wildcat's butt with a hot poker than not let us go." But he just snatched up on our ears a little harder and told us to pay attention while his wife screamed at us some more.

I watched Jason ease the lighter toward the fuses, and the woman's voice just seemed to fade away as me and Jason both started laughing. Well, of course, this just aggravated the man that much more. He looked down at me and said, "At what point are you gonna realize that I'm the big dog here and you're gonna respect my wife and listen to what she's saying?"

It was about then that those rockets went to screaming and popping and exploding. That guy let go of us and started running around more confused than a five-legged cat trying to cover crap on a marble floor. Jason and I broke free and were outta there faster than a blind dog in a dodgeball game. We looked back and saw the man's overalls had caught fire and he was on his butt, sliding across the ground, trying to put out the flames.

When we got halfway across the field, we couldn't run anymore, 'cause we were laughing so hard watching him. He finally got back to his feet and was hog-tied and pigeon-toed all at the same time. It was obvious he was hotter than the hinges of hell on a Halloween night, and he was yelling for us to come back. He was picking up parts of Run Over Rover and slinging them toward us. I yelled back at him, "Next Saturday—same time, same place. But remember: this is a dog-eat-dog world, so don't come around here wearin' no Milk-Bone underwear!"

Me and Jason grabbed our bikes and ducked into the woods, knowing that next Saturday we were definitely sleeping in.

[Ronosophy]

1. It's hard to have a battle of wits with an unarmed person.

2. If life was fair, the horse would get to ride half the time.

3. There's a big difference between dancing with the devil . . . and sleeping with him.

4. Beating a dead horse don't make it taste any better.

5. No matter how you dress a pig, it's still a pig.

6. Remember: the Ark was built by amateurs; the *Titanic* was built by professionals.

7. Men are like bank accounts: if they ain't got no money, they don't get much interest.

8. You have to be 10 percent smarter than the equipment you're driving.

9. Even a blind hog can find an acorn every now and then.

10. Some days you're the dog that caught the car.

11. You go to hell as fast for lying as you do for stealing chickens.

12. Opinions are like buttholes: some are just louder and smellier than others.

13. A day without sunshine is like . . . night.

14. A bumblebee is always faster than the tractor you're driving.

15. If there's one rat you can see, there's fifty you can't.

16. When you plant a tater, you'll only get a tater.

2

Letting the Cat Out of the Bag . . . Is a Whole Lot Easier Than Putting Him Back In

When we were coming along, my pops took great pleasure in being more aggravating than an army of jock-itch ants. He was one of the few people I've ever met who could drive a wooden Indian out of his mind. He especially got a thrill out of annoying my younger sister, Sandy.

Since we never did have money to buy pets, we caught or dug up everything we ever raised. One Easter, Sandy wanted a pet rabbit more than anything in the world. And even though Sandy is usually diagonally parked in a parallel universe, me and Jason wanted to make her Easter wish come true. So we spent every afternoon for a week after school building homemade rabbit boxes. We were busier than a stump full of smoked ants. We figured we'd put them out Friday night, then take Sandy with us Easter Sunday morning to check them, in the hopes we'd catch one and she'd be happier than a horsefly trapped in an outhouse.

Well, as Pops was prone to do, he found a way to throw a wrench into our plans. We didn't know it at the time, but Pops had caught an old, wild tomcat in the barn earlier in the week. Now, he knew me and Jason and Sandy would be checking those traps Sunday morning, so he went out Saturday night and loaded one up with that ol' tomcat. I guess he figured we'd open it up right there on the spot and that crazy cat would be on us faster than a crackhead on his pipe. He knew that ol' cat would be wilder than a two-mouth bass at an earthworm family reunion.

Now, our momma always told us the early bird gets the worm, but the persistent bird finds the feeder. So after a whole week of building traps, we knew Easter morning we'd get Sandy her rabbit. Me and Jason and Sandy got up before church and went to see if God had answered our prayers. Now, I've learned that God is sometimes slicker than hot snot on a goat's glass eyeball, and though we don't understand why, He always gives us what we need— even if it's not exactly what we want.

So there we were, heading to the rabbit boxes with about as much gracefulness as three blind Rottweilers at a china factory. All of a sudden, Sandy started screaming like her hair was on fire and her tail was catching. She'd noticed that the door on one of the boxes was down, which meant we had caught ourselves Peter Cottontail. Luggin' the box between us, we high-tailed it back to the shed behind the house faster than a jackrabbit on moonshine. We got inside, locked the door, and went over to the makeshift cage we had built for Sandy's little Easter bunny. Then we pulled the door of the rabbit box open so he could hop on in.

When that ol' tomcat shot out of that box, we were more surprised than a blind dog under a treed raccoon! That ol' cat went to hissing and showing his teeth, his hair standing up on his back like he'd just been blow-dried by a Hoover. Thinking the cat was rabid, I told Jason to sit tight while I ran to get my gun to smoke that ol' cat like wet pine straw at a trash burning.

It was about then that Sandy went to screaming and crying and begging us not to put that ol' stray out of his misery. She looked sadder than a sow that had just lost her slop trough, so me and Jason agreed we wouldn't hurt him.

She even talked us into helping her try to tame that yellow fur ball, because she said everybody gets Easter bunnies but she was the only girl around with an Easter *cat-bunny!*

We devised a plan to keep him in the shed and sneak him table scraps every chance we got. Now, we should've caught on pretty quick when Pops kept asking us what we caught. We told him "Nothing," but he wouldn't let it go.

I guess at that age the intellect is rivaled only by garden tools, and Pops kept saying, "Did you check the trap by the big rock? I know there are rabbits around there."

Finally, after the entire ride to church and we hadn't let on we had us a cat-bunny, Pops said, "What did y'all do with that cat I slipped in that trap?"

Now, right then you could bar the doors and tie down the stools, 'cause Pops went and told on himself! Momma was madder than a cowboy at a fashion show. She started in on him for putting the cat in there; me and Jason was mad he had planned on letting that ol' pole cat tear into us like a great white shark at a sushi bar; and Sandy was bawling because she knew Pops didn't like cats and he was gonna make her let it go.

So after ten minutes of riding the old man like a borrowed Corvette, to make everyone happy, Pops said we could keep the cat. We decided to name him Wildman and set out to make him not only tame, but part of the family. Of course, if he was gonna be part of the Shirley clan, he'd better get used to Pops aggravating him.

After a few weeks, we had somewhat domesticated that ol' feline, and we were outside playing when Pops came to the front yard and asked us if we knew what a sandwich was. We just looked at him like he was a few fries short of a Happy Meal. He smiled and said, "Well, I just invented a cat-wich!" Sandy's eyes bugged out like a toady frog in a hailstorm. Then she looked around Pops and saw Wildman buried from the neck down in the sandbox.

A few days after that, we came home and couldn't find Wildman anywhere, so Sandy asked Pops where he was.

"He's probably just hangin' out," he told her. We knew we'd better find him quick, and sure enough, we found Wildman hanging on the clothesline dripping wet, his back feet tied together. Sandy was mad enough to stump whip chitlins. See, Pops had made up his mind that he was gonna get this cat to leave or aggravate us enough to give it away, but Sandy is more stubborn than a harnessed Sunday pack mule—and that cat wasn't backin' down none either.

A few Saturdays later, we were having some friends over and Pops walked by us outside and said, "Y'all wanna see a magic trick?"

Of course, we were more excited than a hockey player with his first fake tooth, so we all chimed in, "Yes!"

Well, just outside our house is a huge old cedar tree, about twenty feet tall. Pops reached down, grabbed that cat, and slung him like a Babe Ruth pop fly right up to the top of that tree. "Look," he said, "I made a cat disappear!"

I don't know if that cat just liked the tree, or if he took that toss personally, but he set up a permanent residence right there in those thick branches, and from then on that's where you'd find him. I guess he'd also been taking all those weeks of aggravation to heart, 'cause from then on anyone could walk by that tree but Pops. If Pops came by that cedar tree, ol' Wildman would pounce out quicker than a three-armed tobacco picker on a hot day looking for a glass of ice water. He'd claw that man's legs all to pieces and then run right back up into that tree.

In fact, this started becoming a daily occurrence. It was

like that cat would just sit and wait. And since the tree was right outside the front door, we used to sit on the porch and wait for Pops to get home, just to see which one of them would be slicker than snot over smashed bananas and win the battle of wills that day.

Finally, Pops got smart and started keeping a garden rake at the door. When he'd go to his truck, he'd run that cat back under the tree with the rake, and then he'd toss it in the back of the truck for when he came home. Well, that ol' cat was a quick learner. It didn't take him too many times being in the Kool-Aid to guess the flavor. Pops, being Pops, also never could leave well enough alone. So one evening, he came home, and we were sitting on the porch. Pops went to walk by that tree and out jumped ol' Wildman. Pops ran him back under the tree with that rake, but then he started beating all the lower branches, screaming at the cat and trying to flag him out. We knew right then that was gonna go over like a pregnant pole-vaulter. Sandy started screaming at Pops, Momma ran out to see what Sandy was screaming about, Pops was yelling at the cat—and me and Jason were just dying with laughter.

It was at that point that I saw my first cat-bird. As Pops kept beating that tree, me and Jason saw Wildman leap out from the top. He had climbed all the way up and launched himself, but he wasn't heading to the open ground. He had a spot already marked: he landed right on top of Pops's head and latched on to it like a big-nosed mosquito at a blood bank.

Pops threw his rake down and went to running around, scared as a sinner in a cyclone. Wildman was hissing and biting, and Pops was beating himself half to death trying to get that cat to turn loose! There was a small bucket filled with rainwater that we always left out for the animals to drink—Pops grabbed hold of that bucket and doused his own head! Wildman jumped to the ground . . . but he wasn't done. He started in on Pops's leg like a duck on a June bug, and Pops, having been disarmed and now rakeless, broke into a run down the driveway screaming for Momma to help. Ol' Wildman was in hot pursuit, chasing Pops and hissing. I swear I ain't never seen my dad run so fast! He was moving faster than ice cream at a Jenny Craig convention, and all you could see were feet and yellow fur as Pops was screaming, "Judy, get this damn cat! Judy, help! Judy . . . Judy, help me!"

All three of us looked at Momma to see what she was gonna do. She just smiled and said, "That oughtta teach him that lettin' the cat outta the bag is a whole lot easier than putting him back in." And with that, she went back inside.

I never did ask Pops how far he ran that day, but he and that cat had a come-to-Jesus meeting. From then on, Wildman stayed on the porch and Pops never messed with him again.

[Women & Marriage]

1. There's two theories about arguing with a woman . . . and neither one of 'em works.

2. I can't complain. I'm married and my wife don't listen no more.

3. There's two people in a marriage: one's always right and the other's always the husband.

4. The only thing that separates her from white trash is her rich husband.

5. I knew I married Miss Right. I just didn't know her first name was "Always."

[Surprise]

1. Butter my butt and call me a biscuit!

2. Well, dip me in honey and throw me to the lesbians!

3. Now, don't that just dill your pickle!

4. I'll be hog-tied and pigeon-toed.

5. Her jaw dropped so far you could put forty dollars' worth of ten-cent gumballs in there.

[Unlikely]

1. You'd have a better chance of finding a diamond in a billy goat's butt.

2. You'd have a better chance of finding a feather on a frog.

3. I'd have a better chance of freezing moonshine.

3

Tell Me What You Need . . . And I'll Tell You How to Get Along Without It

There are a few things in life that you never forget; things that stick with you like stink on a billy goat. Most folks never forget their first car, their first kiss, or their first fight, and everyone remembers their first puppy.

When we grew up, me and Jason were so poor we had to ride double on our stick horse, so there was no way Pops was ever gonna spend money on a dog. He always told us we'd go out and get us a sooner—which, to him, meant the dog would sooner be this than that; but we always wanted a dog with a pedigree (even though, at the time, we just thought that meant he ate fancy dog food and had the right to wear a collar). Me and Jason figured the only way we were ever gonna get a real dog was to buckle down and start earning our own money to buy one, since we knew we'd rather be chewing on buttholes than to ask Pops for any money to spend on a dog.

At the time, the big sensation was pit bulls. Every kid around had one and they would tie an ol' lead rope on the dog's neck and prance them jewels up and down the roads, high-stepping like a rooster in wool socks. So we decided we was gonna get us one of them pit bulls—even though everybody told us they were the meanest dogs on the planet and we would rather go skinny-dipping in a fifty-five-gallon barrel of calf slobber than to own one. So we did what all kids who loved their dad and respected his opinion would do: We went straight to Momma for permission.

Now, Momma always told us to ride hard, shoot straight, and tell the truth. And we didn't mind doing that . . . as long as Pops didn't find out. So we told her we wanted to work all summer in the tobacco fields and do odd jobs on the weekends to get us enough money to buy a pit bull. Momma thought this idea made as much sense as putting a screen door on a submarine. She didn't understand why we wanted a dog with such a vicious reputation; she was dead-set against it. Me and Jason knew convincing her would be harder than pulling fly poop from a pepper shaker, but we also knew with a few "pleases" and a lot of tears we could convince her. Then she'd convince Pops.

After two weeks or so of constant badgering, she finally gave in and told us if we could raise the money by the end of summer she'd talk to Pops. Of course, she knew as well as we did, if you're gonna drive cattle through town, do it on a Sunday when there's less traffic and fewer people to fight. She decided she wasn't gonna tell Pops unless we raised all the money first. We had no quarrels about that. So me and Jason started working right away and continued working all summer long.

We learned two things that summer: First, those farmers will work a young kid harder than a ten-year-old government mule; and second, two can live as cheaply as one—if one of 'em doesn't eat. So we kept every dime we made that summer. We didn't go to any movies; we didn't buy any baseball cards; we didn't even go to the store for our weekly Pepsi and Moon Pie. We put every single cent we made aside.

At the end of the summer we took all our money out and

counted it. Then we looked through the ads in the Sunday paper with Momma to see if we had enough. I'll tell you one thing: people sure are proud of their dogs. Reading those ads in the Sunday paper made us think some of these dog owners were more proud of their pit bulls than a camel jockey with a three-humped camel. We scanned every ad, and with each one, we got to feeling lower than a snake's belly in a wheel rut. Then, in the last ad, we saw that someone was selling registered pit bulls and the price was exactly the amount we had saved up! Jason and I were both as happy as a short-legged, fat pony in a high field of oats.

We reminded Momma that she had to hold up her end of the bargain and get Pops on board with the plan. 'Course, we knew this was gonna be harder than three-day-old snot on an oven door . . . but we also knew Pops would rather be pecked to death by a beakless rooster than to cross Momma. So we went ahead and started thinking of names for our new pit-bull puppy. Well, by the time Momma was done with Pops, he looked like he'd been eaten by bears and crapped over a cliff. We were grinning from ear-to-ear when we heard him make that phone call and set us up an appointment to look at the puppies.

The trip took about an hour, and the whole way there Pops just kept telling us we'd rather grab a wildcat by the tail with our teeth than to own one of these dogs—that they weren't nothing but trouble. But his words were falling on deaf ears and he knew it. Finally, we arrived at the end of this long dirt driveway and turned off the main road. Now, I've always been taught to know how well country people are doing by looking at their barns, not their houses. As we drove down this driveway, every barn I saw had fallen in and there was more trash blowing around than at an abandoned trailer park after a tornado. But I might as well have been pulling up to the White House, 'cause we were getting a pit bull.

When we got to the end of the road there was this old, single-wide trailer. One end of it was jacked up about six feet in the air, and most of the underpinning was missing. This old man came out of the door wearing nothing but a pair of faded overalls, and he was holding his teeth in his hand. Right behind him was what I reckon to be his wife. She was a very healthy woman; in fact, I think that was the VCR she had on her hip for a beeper!

The old man put his teeth in, then stuck out the same hand for me to shake. "Hey, I'm Roland—and these here are Roland's bulls." He pointed to a pen that looked like it was put together with tin cans and electric wire.

Now, it wasn't bad enough I had to shake this guy's hand ('cause, with Pops standing there, I'd rather go skinny dipping in a pool full of porcupines than to disrespect someone); but then, when I looked in that pen, there were six of the mangiest mutts I'd ever seen. Every one of them puppies looked like they suffered from zackly disease: Their heads looked zackly like their butts.

To top it off, the old guy's wife was on him like a green worm on a tomato plant from the second those two came out of that trailer. It was quickly obvious, however, that he was a master at selective hearing, and he just went on like she wasn't even there. She kept saying, "Roland, if one of those mutts gets out after my cats again, I'm gonna shoot 'em."

The old man just ignored her and went on telling us about the dogs.

Well, Pops was looking at me, and I was looking at Jason, and both of us had eyes on the door of Pops's old truck, itchin' to get outta there. But Pops is more stubborn than a harnessed mule and he was dead-set on making us ride this one out.

Ol' Roland stepped inside that pen and you'd have thought someone had thrown a big ol' steak bone in there. The two biggest pups went after each other like two June bugs on an electric nightlight. They were tearing each other apart! They rolled into the doghouse and sounded like two tin skeletons in a Texas tornado. Roland dove into that doghouse headfirst after them and, faster than you can skin a flathead catfish, one of the dogs came flying out and landed across the pen. Roland crawled out of the doghouse, smiled, and said, "Dogs will be dogs." That's when we all noticed that he didn't have any bottom teeth. Then the other pup came out of the doghouse—with Roland's teeth sticking out of his mouth, grinning like a steamed raccoon!

Suddenly, Roland realized his teeth were running across the pen—and so did the other pup. Before you could blink, the three of them were chomping around after each other like they were playing Pac-Man. Roland grabbed one dog by the neck and snatched him up faster than a whore's drawers on Sunday morning. He yanked his lower set of teeth from the dog's jaw and chucked him outside the fence. That ol' pup must've known he was in trouble 'cause he went and crawled up under Pops's truck.

None of us three had yet to say a word. Roland yelled to his wife to grab the puppy so we could look at it, and she started trying to crawl under the truck. It wasn't bad enough that she was so big the only thing we could see was her bohaunkus, which looked like two Buicks fighting for a parking place while she was trying to get under that truck, but she was also so ugly she had to sneak up on a glass of water to drink it. I don't know if that puppy was as scared of the view as I was, but I was ready to leave. Unfortunately, we weren't going anywhere until that pup was out from under Pops's truck.

While this was going on, Roland was screaming at his wife, she was screaming at the dog, and the dog was yelping (because she must've been tuggin' on its leg or ear). In the middle of all this commotion, an old, three-legged cat came hobbling by. Now, I don't know if this cat was deaf or just plain dumb, but as soon as that dog under the truck saw it, he set off after that cat like a brown cow on chocolate milk. He ran that old fleabag right under the trailer and up an old piece of flexible duct tape that was hanging down. As that cat ran by us on his way to cover, I could see he was already missing an ear and an eye, and his tail was half chewed off.

All at once the old woman started screaming so loud it curled the ears on every dog out there. Roland just took his hat off, sat down on an old stump, and started scratching his head. She was yelling, "Roland, I'm gonna git my gun and kill that mangy dog of yours! I done warned you if they messed with my cats again I was gonna kill 'em graveyard dead!" Then she took off for the house and came flying back out with a big ol' pistol! She started crawling under the trailer, giving us a view that was just way too much pumpkin for a nickel. She cussed and screamed at that dog—I hadn't ever heard words like she used. You could've grown potatoes in her dirty mouth.

Meanwhile, the cat was howling and clawing and we saw the dog come dragging it out by one of its three legs, shaking his head back and forth the whole time. The woman was screaming and trying to aim the pistol, when suddenly the gun went off and the dog went limp.

She crawled out from under that trailer with what looked like a regurgitated fur ball in her hands. "You see that, Roland! They done killed another one!" She stormed back in the trailer and slammed the door behind her.

Roland looked up at Pops and said, with the straightest face I've ever seen, "The dead one's free and I still got five live ones to choose from, if you're interested."

Pops's jaw dropped so far you could've put forty dollars' worth of ten-cent gumballs in it. He just smiled and said, "Roland, we'll think about it."

By that time, me and Jason were already back in the truck. As we drove back out the driveway, Pops said, "Well, what do you boys want next?" Me and Jason knew this was usually the warm-up for the "I told you so" speech. But the only other thing Pops said on the way home was, "From now on, boys, when you have bright ideas, just come to me first and tell me what you need. Then I'll tell you how to get along without it."

[Hot]

1. Hotter than a hooker in the front row of a Sunday service.
2. Hotter than forty acres of burning stumps.
3. Hotter than nine miles of Alabama asphalt on a Talladega Sunday.
4. Hotter than the hinges of hell on Halloween night.
5. Hotter than two hamsters farting in a wool sock.
6. Hotter than a goat's butt in a jalapeño pepper patch.
7. Hotter than a billy goat with a blowtorch.
8. Hotter than a hooker's doorknob on payday.
9. Hotter than a pot of collards on the back burner of a four-dollar stove.
10. Hotter than a two-dollar pistol at an all-night shootout.
11. Hotter than a two-peckered billy goat.
12. Hotter than a four-balled tomcat.
13. Hotter than a blistered pecker in a wool sock in a sauna.
14. Sexier than socks on a billy goat.
15. She's so hot I'd crawl naked up a mountain of broken glass just to hear her piss in a tin can over a walkie-talkie.
16. Hotter than a pig roast at Satan's house.
17. Hot enough to melt bronze in an ice storm.
18. Hotter than a gasoline-dipped hen at a chicken roast.
19. Hotter than a June bride in a feather bed.

[Slick]

1. Slicker than snot over smashed bananas.
2. Slicker than a harpooned hippo in a banana tree.
3. Slicker than the devil in velvet pants in a pool of baby oil.
4. Slicker than a hound's fake tooth.
5. Slicker than grease in a barbecue biscuit.
6. Slick as a three-legged dog trying to cover crap on an ice-covered pond.
7. Slicker than snot on a glass doorknob.
8. Slicker than cat crap on greased linoleum.
9. Slicker than a skinned Georgia catfish soaked in baby oil.

[Mouthy]

1. Her mouth is dirtier than a boardinghouse toilet.
2. She could suck a golf ball through a twenty-foot garden hose with a mouth like that.
3. She's got enough mouth for four sets of teeth.
4. She could suck the feathers off a duck with a mouth like that.
5. You could grow potatoes in that dirty mouth.
6. You couldn't melt butter in that mouth.

4

Trains and Trouble

When I was younger, my parents always took me and my brother to Topsail Island for summer vacation. Now, money was as scarce as feathers on a toad in those days, so once we got there we spent most of our time on the beach or the pier instead of at the arcade. Well, this one particular summer they let me take a buddy of mine named Shane with us. We spent all morning on the pier, but the fishing was so bad we couldn't have caught a cold naked in the deep-freeze that day. So we started devising other ways to entertain ourselves.

Now, Shane was a great guy, but at times he was so dumb you'd have to water him. And my intellect back in those days was such that, if brains were dynamite, I couldn't blow my nose. So usually I followed right along with his plans. Well, we got to noticing all the seagulls at the end of the pier and the people throwing them Cheetos. Those birds would come down, practically eat out of their hands, and then fly away. This gave Shane a brilliant idea. He said, "Let's go under the pier, take the fishing rods, and put some Cheetos on the hooks. Then we can catch us a seagull and fly him like a kite!"

Even though that made about as much sense to me as giving a grizzly bear a backrub with a handful of razor blades, I had to admit it would be pretty cool to have a live kite, so I was all over his idea like a hobo on a ham sandwich. We scoured the pier and found some chips and Cheetos, and then headed out to do a little "fly" fishing.

We got set up, gave about a twenty-yard buffer from where we set the bait, and hid with a rod in hand behind one of the pier legs. Didn't take but a few minutes before a gull swooped down and jumped on that Cheeto like a monkey in a banana warehouse. So there we were, with our live kite about fifty yards in the air, thinking this was the coolest thing since ice cream, when a huge crowd gathered on the pier. About that time we both realized that maybe we didn't think this thing through, so we started trying to reel that gull in with the intention of letting him go and getting our tails on outta there. Problem was, the gull was stronger than our reel and all he was doing was pulling drag. Shane started yelling at me, I started yelling at the bird, and everyone on the pier started yelling at us. That's when I saw the blue lights coming down the beach.

The cops rolled up in a four-by-four jeep and jumped out, heading straight for us. They looked madder than wet hornets. One of them yelled, "Do you kids know it's a five-thousand-dollar fine to harass seagulls out here?"

With that, Shane was off like a prom dress, and I was nervous as a dog crapping peach pits. One cop broke out after Shane and the other threw me into the sand and slapped on the handcuffs. He wasn't no small cop either; in fact, he was fatter than an outhouse spider. So when he picked me up and slammed me on the hood of the jeep, I assure you he was about as gentle as a peach-orchard boar in a patch of strawberries.

So there I was, lying on the hood of the patrol jeep looking down the beach, scared as a whore in the front row at church about what Pops was gonna do to me, when I saw the other cop hauling Shane back to the jeep. Problem was,

Shane didn't have his britches on! In his quest for freedom, he had tried to swim for it. I don't know where he thought he was gonna go, but there wasn't a lot of chlorine in his gene pool. Shane told me later that when he jumped in the water, he figured the cop wouldn't follow—and he was right. The cop just stood on the shore knowing he had to come back . . . because he had nowhere to go. After a few minutes of treading water, Shane had the same epiphany and headed back to shore. But when he had nosedived into that water like a skeeter in a tailspin at a blood bank, he'd lost his swimming shorts. Unfortunately, it was colder that day than my mother-in-law's heart, and there's Shane free-balling it! I was covered in sand, with my face pretty bloodied up from the gentleness of the good cop, and everyone on the pier was laughing and clapping.

We both got loaded into the back of the jeep, headed for jail. I just knew when Pops got a hold of us he was gonna stomp a mud hole in our butts and then walk it dry. But Shane managed to find humor in the situation. He said, "You know, Ronnie, you can pick your friends and you can pick your boogers, but you can't wipe your friends on your seat." I just sat there petrified as to what was about to happen.

After Pops bailed us out, we got in his car and no one said a word. We drove about five minutes before Pops spoke. And when he finally did, all he said was, "Son, from now on, remember: When you think you have a brilliant idea, the light at the end of the tunnel is usually the headlight of the oncoming train."

Looking back, Pops always had a way of giving good advice. And since that day, I've spent much of my life trying to avoid trains—and trouble.

[You're My Kind of People If . . .]

1. You're so country, your diploma reads SCHOOL OF TAXIDERMY.
2. You'd rather dip yourself in honey and jump into a bear's den.
3. You see a turtle on a fence post and can't figure out how he got there himself.
4. You know women are like artichokes; you have to go through so much to get so little.
5. You're born an original and don't die a copy.
6. You were so poor when you were young, your momma put a loaf of bread on layaway.
7. You're slicker than whale crap on an ice floe.
8. You're tougher than a woodpecker's lips dipped in cement.
9. You're so backwoods, you chapped your lips on the cow's udders getting milk.
10. You're so redneck, you're Appalachian American.
11. You've got more sense in your pocket than your head.
12. You're surrounded by the absence of sophistication and an abundance of ignorance.
13. Your family tree has only one limb and it's broken.
14. You're as useless as an ashtray on a motorcycle.
15. You didn't fall off the turnip truck—your parents did!
16. You make Forrest Gump sound articulate.
17. You lost your tongue trying to open up a can of Copenhagen.
18. You're slicker than a greased pig on a Mongolian barbecue.

19. You're slower than Stephen Hawking in a blizzard.
20. You'd give me change back if I asked you for two cents.

5

Chasing Your Tail Gets You Nowhere Except Back to Where You Started

When it comes to animals, my daddy loves them more than he loves his people. If you mess with Pops's animals, he gets madder than a blind man at a nude beach.

When we were growing up, they'd have twenty-nine-cent hamburgers at Hardee's every Tuesday. The cheeseburgers were thirty-nine cents. My daddy would take us to Hardee's and he'd refuse to spend the extra dime for cheese. Pops would always tell us we could put cheese on them when we got home. I mean, Pops was so tight at times, I've seen him squeeze blood out of the eyes on a penny. But every week, Pops would still buy ten hamburgers and ten cheeseburgers. As soon as we walked out of Hardee's, Pops would unwrap the cheeseburgers and throw them to the two dogs in the back of his truck. That always made me and Jason hotter than a wildcat in a forest fire with an overcoat on.

That's just the way Pops is about animals. Whenever Pops cooks steaks, his dogs are eating steaks on the floor before we even get our plates. When it comes to his animals, I truly believe Pops loves them more than he loves his own family. But they are always there for him. See, Pops is a hard man to get along with, and he's more stubborn than the northern end of a southern-bound pack mule, and them critters can't talk back.

Of course, Pops's favorite pet was always Wildman, the stray cat we caught in the rabbit trap and gave to my sister.

Even though Wildman hated Pops and used to attack him as soon as he climbed out of his car, Pops learned to love the cat over time. Even though Wildman would attack Pops like a one-legged man at IHOP, their hatred for each other really became their bond. It became a chess game between the two. It would take Pops five minutes to get from his car to the house, because Wildman was always hiding in places and waiting for him just like a kid. It was the funniest thing you ever saw. A grown man running from a tomcat looking as scared as a blind mouse in a rattlesnake pit is an image I'll never forget.

Eventually, Pops wouldn't let you mess with Wildman. I remember one day when my grandfather saw Wildman attack Pops. Grandpaw picked up the cat and said, "Y'all want to see this cat disappear? Best magic trick I know." We all nodded our heads in excitement. The closest thing we'd ever seen to magic was Mickey Mouse on a cartoon. Grandpaw picked up that cat by the back of the neck and swung him into the top of a tree. He said, "Look boys, he disappeared." Bo, my daddy jumped on my grandfather like nothing you've ever seen. He was like a Viking in a panty raid. It was then we knew we'd better never mess with Wildman.

One day when Pops came home from work, he climbed out of his car and started looking around for Wildman. The cat didn't attack him. He walked into the backyard, and Wildman never attacked him. He walked inside the house and still couldn't find Wildman. Pops was starting to get worried; he looked like a banker at an IRS audit. Wildman never came out, and you could tell it was really bothering Pops. He started getting mad at us, thinking we'd done something to the cat, like we'd locked him in the shed or something. Pops was madder than a bobcat in a forest fire.

"Pops, I swear we haven't done anything to him," I told him.

Pops sent us outside to find Wildman. We looked in the sheds outside, under the porch, in the woods, and everywhere else. We couldn't find him. But then I saw a big orange spot at the end of the driveway, right next to the road that runs in front of my parents' house. I didn't wanna go see what it was and I sure didn't wanna go tell my pops. I'd rather jump in a five-gallon bucket of armpits off a ten-foot ladder, but I was the oldest and it was my duty.

Pops saw the cat lying at the end of the driveway. Now, my daddy is a man's man—he never cries or get upset. But I'm telling you, he was torn up over losing that cat. To this day, I can still remember the look of sadness on his face. He was more upset than Kirstie Alley when McDonald's runs out of French fries. I'd never seen my father that upset. I worried he was going to have a heart attack over a dead cat. Pops looked like a dead pig in sunshine.

I went to the shed, got a shovel, and picked up Wildman. We brought him into the backyard, and Pops made Jason and me dig the cat a grave. We went inside the house and built a small wooden box for Wildman's casket, and put pictures of Pops and the cat in the box. Then we went into the backyard and had a full funeral service for Wildman and buried him in front of a small tree. Pops even wrote a eulogy for Wildman and etched an epitaph on a piece of plywood for a tombstone. It said: OUR BATTLE MAY BE OVER BUT THE WAR WILL RAGE ON. YOU'LL NEVER BE FORGOTTEN YOU WORTHLESS CUR. I guess he had to make it seem manly, but we never spoke a word.

It took us two hours to bury the stupid cat. By the time we were finished, I was happier than a bullfrog at a blowfly convention. I would have taken that cat down the road and thrown it into a lake. I love animals, but an animal is still an animal. A two-hour funeral for a cat was about as much fun as a nosebleed.

For the next two days, you couldn't speak to my father. It was like Pops lost a kid. He was so torn up about it. Pops would come home and sit in his car for thirty minutes. It was almost like he was out there waiting for Wildman to attack him.

The following weekend, Jason and I got up early because we were going to go fishing. I tried to get Pops to go fishing with us.

"Pops, I know you've been upset," I told him. "Why don't you come along with us?"

"Nah, I don't want to go fishing," he said.

I kept pestering Pops to go because I was really getting worried about how upset he was at losing Wildman.

Pops finally agreed to go with us. We walked outside to get our fishing poles and tackle box out of the shed. Then we climbed into our little Ford Ranger. Now, the Ranger was only used on the weekends, for things like hauling trash off or heading to the fishing hole. So we hadn't been in it for a few days—as a matter of fact, since the day before Wildman went missing.

I was driving, Jason was sitting in the middle, and Pops was sitting on the passenger's side. About the time Pops sat down, Wildman jumped out of nowhere and climbed onto his head. That cat locked onto his head like Rosie O'Donnell locks onto a turkey leg. It was like somebody had dipped a hamburger in honey and thrown it to the bumblebees.

Wildman hadn't seen Pops in four days and now he was getting his money's worth. Jason and I couldn't help Pops because we were in shock because we thought the cat was dead. We were like, "Where did this cat come from?"

But Pops was happier than a two-tongued toad in a room full of fireflys. He was trying to rub and love the cat, but Wildman was just scratching up his head and face. By the time Wildman was done with him, Pops's face looked like it had caught on fire and somebody tried to put it out with steel-toed cleats. He was bleeding from head to toe.

Wildman eventually jumped out of the truck and ran off into the woods. Pops was jumping up and down and screaming, "Judy! Judy! Wildman is back!"

I had never seen my daddy that happy. He looked like a two-headed mule in a one-hundred-acre hay field.

We were supposed to be going fishing, but Pops ran into the shed and came back with two shovels. He handed them to Jason and me and told us to move the rocks off the grave, and to dig up the box and open it. Pops wanted to make sure there was still a cat in the grave because he just knew Wildman had come back from the dead. It was like a scene out of *Pet Sematary*. Pops swore that his cat had come back from the grave.

Jason and I started digging, but we were so mad. We were hotter than a toothless dog in a sausage factory. We dug up the box and sat down. By then, the box smelled like somebody had licked the butthole of a skunk after three or four days. The box was just rancid. We opened the box and sure enough there was still a cat inside it.

To this day, if you ask Pops about Wildman, he still swears it was a reincarnation. But I know there are two certainties in life—cats don't come back to life and chasing your tail gets you nowhere, except back to where you started.

[You'd Rather . . .]

1. You'd rather jump off a five-foot ladder into a ten-gallon bucket of porcupines.

2. You'd rather be superglued to the Tasmanian Devil in a phone booth.

3. You'd rather slide down a mountain of razor blades naked into a swimming pool of alcohol.

4. You'd rather be duct-taped to a bar of soap on the shower floor of a men's prison.

5. You'd rather have a knife fight with Freddy Krueger in a phone booth.

6. You'd rather drink five gallons of gas and piss on a forest fire.

7. You'd rather be pecked to death by a rooster with a rubber beak.

8. You'd rather be chewing buttholes off of skunks.

9. You'd rather give a grizzly bear a backrub with a handful of razor blades.

10. You'd rather have hemorrhoids the size of grapefruits.

11. You'd rather stare at the sun through a set of high-powered binoculars.

12. You'd rather fight a tiger with a switch in the dark.

13. You'd rather be hog-tied to a grizzly bear fresh up from hibernation.

14. You'd rather eat a cold scab sandwich and drink a glass of green snot.

15. You'd rather shove a wet noodle up a wildcat's tail with a hot poker.

16. You'd rather rub the hair off a bobcat's tail with sandpaper in a bathtub.

17. You'd rather pound salt up your tail with a steel brush.

18. You'd rather be a Russian racehorse at the Kentucky Derby with a busted leg and a glue truck on your tail.

19. You'd rather ride a tornado through an ape pen wearing banana underwear.

20. You'd rather be poked in the eye with a blunt stick.

21. You'd rather go fart peas at the new moon.

22. You'd rather grab a wildcat by the tail with your teeth.

23. You'd rather skinny-dip in a pool of piranhas.

24. You'd rather be super-glued to a tornado in an Oklahoma pigpen.

25. You'd rather wear pork-chop panties and run through a lion's den.

26. You'd rather pole-vault over a barbed-wire fence with a rubber stick.

27. You'd rather be a short-legged rooster in a high-water hog pen.

28. You'd rather be superglued to a chimpanzee with a blowtorch in a room full of dynamite.

29. You'd rather be chained to the underbelly of a moose during mating season.

30. You'd rather light a match in a room full of old grandma fart bags.

31. You'd rather dip yourself in honey and throw yourself on a nest of fire ants.

32. You'd rather jump out of an airplane tied to a cinder block.

33. You'd rather swim with great whites after bathing in razor blades.

34. You'd rather slap a kitten at a PETA convention.

6

Go for the Ugly Early . . . And You'll Never Go Home Alone

Back when I was a teenager and more out of control than a racecar with Ray Charles at the wheel, there wasn't a weekend that me, Jason, and our cousin Brian didn't make the hour-long trek down to East Carolina University.

We spent most of our teen years—and all our money—between the bars there. ECU was a young man's playground; the girls down there were hotter than a pig roast at Satan's house, and the only fake things on them were their purses. My pops once said that even a blind hog can find an acorn every now and again; well, down there a dead hog could still root up a whole bushel of 'em!

We all had our fake IDs—and they looked about as real as Joan Rivers's face—but we always got into the clubs just the same. Oddly, it was never the doormen who nailed us on those IDs; it was always the bartenders. When it came to checking everyone every time a drink was bought, they were tighter than a skeeter's tail in a nosedive heading toward a can of OFF. So we started getting innovative and made sure to buy our beer before we went, and to always have a designated driver. By the time we got to the bars, we would already be as tore up as a football bat on a Friday-night light. We learned to let the beer get a little warm before drinking it so we could smuggle the bottle in our drawers and not draw up tight as a horsefly's tail stretched over a fifty-five-gallon drum.

One Friday, I remember we were gonna drive the old

Mercury Grand Marquis owned by one of Jason's friends. That thing was uglier than a monkey's armpit after a snot bath, and it ran about as well as a legless dog. But if we had a chance to get to ECU, then the choices were to backstroke it all the way to the front door or get left behind. So we all decided to pile in and let Jason's buddy do the honors. We packed into that old heap, cranked up some Hank Williams Jr., and got ready to get right until daylight. Brian brought the booze: four individual six-packs (one for me, one for him, one for Jason, and two beers apiece to sneak inside). We never were smokers, but being from the dirty South, there's one thing you could be sure of: we were dippers. Skoal Long Cut Traditional was our dip of choice. Heck, me and Brian had the can rings worn out so bad in our back pockets you could read the expiration dates in the denim! Get me a hot woman, a cold beer, and a new can, and I'd be happier than a hungry baby in a topless bar.

Now, being that we were of the young faction, it didn't take us long to get more bent than a butcher's hook. About fifteen minutes out from ECU we saw a convenience store and figured we all needed to go see a man about a horse— and grab some gum, while we were at it, for when we hit the clubs. When we wheeled into that place, there must've been thirty people inside, and poor Brian was about to explode! So we all decided just to back woods it behind the store.

Well, just about the time we were getting out, who pulled up but the local sheriff! You could just look at this fellow and tell he was meaner than a pit bull's ex-wife. When he stepped out of his car we could see he had one of them old burnt-up faces. He had more wrinkles than a bull elephant's ball sack, and his eyes were real beady—like a possum caught in the headlights of a semi on a downhill run. He had a wad in his jaw, and when he saw us he walked right up and spit on the end of Brian's shoe.

"You boys ain't been drinking, now, have you?"

I could tell ol' Brian's tail drew up tighter than a camel's butt in a sandstorm, so I chimed right in and said, "Naw, sir. Not since we ran out a few miles back."

Well, that ol' fellow actually cracked a smile. He asked, "What about your driver?"

I said, "No, sir. He's more sober than a Sunday morning preacher at a Saturday night prayer service."

He glared at me for a minute and said, "Well, there's two things this world is running short on: common sense and honesty. I can tell you ain't got none of the former, but you're full of the latter, so I'm gonna let you boys go on and have a good time tonight."

Well, I was grinning like a baked possum. And Jason was heading on out behind the store. But it tore Brian up worse than a naked man rollerblading down a hill of razor blades, so he just eased back into the car. I asked him, "Brian, ain't you still gotta see that man about a horse?"

Brian said, "Nope. I'm gonna corral mine right here."

Now, since we was raised in the cut, I knew that meant he was gonna fill up an old bottle and toss it when we got goin' down the road. But I forgot Brian couldn't engineer his way out of a paper bag with a box cutter. We all loaded back up and headed straight for the main strip.

Back on the road, me and Jason each reached up to the front seat to grab another beer out of the six-pack and cracked the lids on them mugs. I said, "Jason, if you go for the ugly early, you won't go home alone." He just smiled and we turned 'em up.

When I brought my bottle down, I could see that Jason's cheeks were still blowed up like a bullfrog in a blender. It was just about that time ol' Brian yelled, "Oh, no!" And I knew what had just happened: Brian had filled that beer bottle to the brim when he was seeing that man about a horse! To keep it from spilling, Brian had put the top back on; and since we didn't keep our beer on ice, it wasn't unusual that the bottle would be a little warm. Jason realized all this at the exact same time I did, while Brian just looked back on us as baffled as Adam on Mother's Day. Needless to say, Jason spewed all over the car . . . and all over me and Brian. If it wasn't bad enough we had beer and Brian's royal fluids everywhere, it turned out this made our sober driver gag and he ended up puking all over the car whatever he had eaten before we left. Jamming on the brakes at seventy miles an hour, he threw us around that big tin can like dead trout on a Ferris wheel. When we finally came to a stop, I jumped out of the car and just stood there, madder than a wet hen at an omelet breakfast. There I was: covered from head to toe with beer and piss and vomit, dripping like a freshly squeezed tea bag.

Everyone was sick. And there was no way we could go into the bars now. To top it off, it was an hour's drive back to the house. We all looked like death warmed over with a side of bread crumbs, and I was more pissed off than a fart trapped in a vacuum cleaner. I pulled the driver out, told him to sit in the back, and I drove that car straight over to a car wash—where I proceeded to drive through with all the windows down!

Now, I had been in a few car washes before—though never with the windows down. Who would've thought that there'd be hot water and burning hot wax in one of those things? I was figuring we'd rather be wet and soapy than ride around smelling like Brian's insides all the way back. Besides, it wasn't my car; I actually thought I was doing

Jason's buddy a favor. About the time that hot water hit us, we were jumping around the inside of that car like a butcher's dog crapping razor blades. And in all the commotion, no one thought to roll the windows up before the brushes started slapping inside the car, beating us like wet cats in a washing machine. Everyone was screaming and yelling, trapped in there like tuna in a can. All I could do was stick my head between my legs and kiss my tail good-bye! Just when I thought it might be over and we were gonna get outta there with our lives, then came the hot wax, burning into me like an old hooker in a dead man's wallet. By the time we realized we should roll the windows up, we were getting rinsed off with cold water and hanging out the windows lookin' like a bag full of wet buttholes. We had burn marks all over our torsos—but we all had that new-car smell!

I started heading down the highway back to the house, and no one would speak. Brian was shaking like a toothless dog at a bear jamboree, and finally he started trying to apologize. Jason stopped him mid-sentence: "Don't say any more! We will never talk about this ever again." He was serious: "If I ever hear one word mumbled about this, I will beat whoever says it so bad that he'll live the rest of his life as useless as a jam sandwich is to a drowning rabbit." He thought a moment before he added, "But there is one thing I will say." We all got quiet. "I know that this event has scarred me for life, but I also know scars are just tattoos with better stories. Ronnie was right when he said, 'If you go for the ugly early, you won't go home alone. Here I am with you three, and y'all are the ugliest fellows I know!"

We all just busted out laughing. I even thought about grabbing another beer. But thinking better of it, I just cranked up Hank and headed on home.

[Crazy]

1. Nuttier than a Porta Potti at a peanut festival.
2. Crazy as a three-eyed dog in a hubcap factory.
3. Crazy as a crack-house rat.
4. Crazier than a bee-stung stallion.
5. Nuttier than pecan pie.
6. Nuttier than five pounds of fruitcake.
7. He's parallel parked in a diagonal universe.
8. Crazier than a corn-fed 'coon on coke.
9. Crazier than a hippie at a hula-hoop convention.

[Yes]

1. Is a pig's rump made of pork?
2. Does a fat puppy hate fast cars?
3. Do fat babies like chocolate cake?
4. Does a one-legged duck swim in a circle?
5. Does a cat got climbing gear?
6. Do rattlesnakes kiss gently?
7. Does Howdy Doody got wooden balls?
8. If the good Lord's willing and the creek don't rise.
9. As much as fat ticks love lazy dogs.
10. That would be the dog that treed the possum.

7
Don't Ever Corner Nuthin' Meaner Than You

When I was in my teenage years my dad lost his job, so we didn't have enough money to have anything but a bad time. All my friends were always bragging about the cool pets they had: pit-bull dogs, registered Rottweilers, high-dollar horses. So I generally would drag anything home that I could tie a rope around to see what kind of pet it would make. Now, Pops would always tell me when I dragged something up that, if you can't race it or take it to bed, don't bring it home. But I always did suffer from selective hearing.

I was over at my buddy's house one day, sitting on the porch—hanging out, bored as a hooker at a funeral—when I happened to look over in the six-foot pine trees that surrounded his backyard. Well, right there, hanging out like Big Juicy in a two-piece, was a raccoon. Bo, I thought, now that would be the dog that treed the possum as far as making me have the coolest pet. So I started trying to convince my buddy to help me. Now, I love my friend 'bout as much as fat ticks love lazy dogs, but sometimes he's as dumb as a cat trying to look pretty at a dog show, and he don't remember plans very well either. Still, I had this all tied up. I would grab a pair of his dad's welding gloves and he would grab a big ol' quilt, and we would surround this critter like he was Custer's horse. I would grab the raccoon and throw him in the blanket, and all my buddy had to do was cover him up.

Well, he wasn't none too convinced that this was a well-thought-out plan, because he was the one that would end up holding the 'coon. But I was the only one tall enough to reach that critter in the top of the tree. So we grabbed our gear and headed over.

Now, the whole time this ol' 'coon had been eyeing us. He looked as confused as a cow on Astroturf and I could tell he was getting a bit antsy. He started turning circles in the top of that little tree. But I knew that when I went for him, he had to be facing away from me so I could toss him directly toward the quilt.

My buddy was standing there with the quilt just below eye level, and he was trying to back out. "Ronnie," he said, "this is gonna go over like a turd in a punch bowl." But I convinced him that we could really land some girls that were hot enough to run a buzzard off a gut barrel at lunchtime if we had a pet 'coon. So I started easing up with all the grace of a blind elephant in a china shop, and that 'coon started making a fuss. I told my buddy to whistle to distract it while I made my move.

Truthfully, I didn't realize how fast 'coons were. Just before I reached him, he set sail. Problem was, he could also jump farther than we had figured. Once that ol' 'coon took off, he was in line to land right on top of my buddy's head. But instead of just simply raising the blanket up and letting the 'coon land in our perfectly devised trap, my buddy threw the quilt on the ground and turned around to run. We had made this 'coon pretty damn mad. So about the time he broke for the tree line through these small pines, whether it was coincidence or just plain meanness I don't know, that 'coon was dead on my buddy's heels. He was on him harder than a twelve-peckered billy goat in mating season, and I couldn't catch neither one of them.

My buddy's running, branches were smacking him in the face, he's screaming for me, the 'coon's on his heels hissing like a three-tongued snake, and there I was in tow trying to save my buddy from a ten-pound critter.

After about a thirty-second dash, the 'coon scaled another small tree. My friend's heart was beating faster than that of a Russian racehorse at the Kentucky Derby with a glue truck behind him. He was cussing and screaming at me, telling me how he was almost killed by a raccoon, and I was trying to convince him to run and grab the quilt 'cause we now had a second chance to capture this rascal.

Well you would have thought I had left his sister at the bowling alley on a Friday night. I saw his eyes light up and I was pretty sure he wouldn't go along this time. He rolled right up on me and I thought he was getting ready to try and lay me out with a haymaker; but instead, he just stood there for about ten seconds, breathing hard, blood pouring from all the scratches on his face, his arms tore all to pieces from the branches. The 'coon was still screeching at us and I was still wanting to grab him. Just then, in a very sincere voice, my buddy said what probably turned out to be some of the best advice anyone could live by. "Ronnie," he said, "I'd fight hell and half of Georgia by your side, and would paddle the life boat if life's creek ever rose on ya. But brother, you want that 'coon, you're gonna have to catch him yourself, 'cause I ain't never gonna try to corner nuthin' meaner than me again." With that, he left me and that 'coon in the woods alone.

After thinking about the situation and looking up at that 'coon staring down on me, madder than a bobcat tied up in a piss fire, I decided that maybe a pet turtle would be just as cool. So I ran after my buddy, hoping I could talk him into going to the pond.

[People]

1. He's so little, he'd have to run around twice to make a shadow.

2. He's so small, he's got only one stripe on his PJs.

3. She's finer than a frog hair split eight ways.

4. He's as graceful as a Sherman tank in a china shop.

5. He's luckier than a Thanksgiving turkey on Christmas Day.

6. He's lower than a mole's belly button on digging day.

7. He's more stubborn than a ten-year-old government mule.

8. She's prettier than a mess of fried catfish.

9. She's smoother than a baby's tail after a waxing.

10. He's smooth as a pig on stilts.

11. He's meaner than a skillet full of rattlesnakes.

12. He's as tore up as a football bat on a Friday-night light.

13. He's wilder than a peach-orchard hog.

14. She smells worse than the outhouse door on a shrimp boat.

15. She's so blind, she'd miss Ray Charles playing cards with a crawdad.

16. She's lower than a snake's belly in a wheel rut.

17. She's as subtle as an unflushed toilet.

18. She'd put a rattlesnake in your pocket then ask you for a light.

19. She's got bees in her bonnet and ants in her pants.

20. That girl's riding a gravy train on biscuit wheels.

21. He looks like the cat that swallowed the canary.

22. He's lower than an ankle bracelet on a flat-footed pygmy.

23. He's worse off than a rubber-nosed woodpecker in a petrified forest.

24. He's like a pet raccoon: he can't seem to keep his hands off anything.

25. He's like a billy goat: hard-headed with a stinkin' tail.

26. He must've learned to whisper in a sawmill.

27. That boy's higher than giraffe nuts.

28. That boy would talk a wooden Indian out of his mind.

29. Too many freaks, not enough circus.

30. He's wilder than a two-mouthed bass at an earthworm family reunion.

31. He was more excited than a hockey player with his first fake tooth.

32. He was prouder than a camel jockey with a three-humped camel.

33. He's more out of control than a racecar with Ray Charles at the wheel.

34. She's got more wrinkles than an elephant's ball sack.

35. He acted like I had left his sister in the bowling alley on a Friday night.

36. Everything he ever learned I think he got from watching *Gilligan's Island*.

37. He couldn't see a set of bull's balls if he was standing between its hind legs.

38. He's stronger than mule piss with the foam farted off.

8

Whoever Said You Can't Buy Happiness Must Have Been Dead Broke

I grew up on a street in Lizard Lick that everybody called Jackass Road. I'm still not exactly sure why it's called that. We never had much money growing up and there wasn't much of anything to do. We were so poor that if we found a quarter, we'd cut it up and divide it into four pieces between us. But there was a junkyard across the street from my parents' house, and Jason and I were always sneaking over there to steal parts off cars to sell. We eventually discovered that in all these old cars were a bunch of *Playboy* magazines. All these old men had dirty magazines in these old cars, so sometimes we'd spend hours over there. We knew we could sell them at school. Like I said, we were so poor our front door was our back one too, and we were definitely early age entrepreneurs.

Jason was always building stuff, so he started making a weekly trip over to the junkyard. He would come back with tire irons, window cranks, and radios—basically whatever he could get out of there. He probably started going over there when he was ten years old, and by the time he was seventeen, we had our own little auto-parts salvage out back. Our backyard looked like Sanford and Son. He decided he was going to build his own car. He was handier than a bear cub playing with itself with mittens on.

On Jason's seventeenth birthday, I told Momma I wanted to throw him a surprise birthday party. I wanted to do something really special for Jason because I love my brother like

Peter loves the Lord. I wanted to do something really cool for him. I told my parents to go out to dinner that night, and I called up all of our buddies. We probably had about ten or twelve guys coming over, and I went out and bought beer and liquor for us. Once the party started cranking, my buddies were more messed up than Lindsay Lohan at a pharmaceutical convention.

What Jason didn't know was that I'd hired him a stripper for the party. It was a big deal because we didn't have much money. When we went to town, the first thing we said was, "We don't want to pay the light bill." It took us forever to pool enough money to pay for a stripper. We probably collected bottles on the side of the road for a month. It was a really big deal. During the two weeks prior to the party, when Jason would wander over to the junkyard, I took Polaroid pictures of him when he wasn't looking.

On the night of the party, I had the stripper meet me up the road. She was hotter than a gasoline cat walking through hell with a kerosene tail. She was dressed as a police officer and looked tighter than two coats of paint. I handed her the photos of Jason in the junkyard and told her the whole story.

She came to the house a few minutes later and pounded on the front door. It was like, *Bam! Bam! Bam!* We opened the door and she yelled out: "Is Jason Shirley here? Is Jason Chad Shirley here?" We were like, "Yeah, he's right there." By that time, Jason was more screwed up than a steel-toed flip-flop. He was looking at her and thinking, "What in the world have I done?" He was more confused than an Amish electrician. She told him, "You're under arrest for breaking and entering and larceny." She started showing him the pictures from the junkyard, and he started sweating and shaking his head. We were all sitting there trying to play it cool and acting all serious. We thought we were slicker than a BP oil spill.

Jason stood up from the couch, and she swung him around and slapped the handcuffs on him. When she slapped the cuffs on him, she was supposed to start dancing. But Jason was more upset than a two-dollar hooker on dollar day. He was upset because he knew Momma and Pops were going to kill him for getting arrested. All of a sudden, Jason yelled, "Heck, no I ain't!" He took off toward the bathroom and dove through a closed window like a seal. He looked like Flipper swimming away from Shamu. He went through that window faster than a cheetah on Amtrak, and it took three or four of us to pull him back into the house.

We were like, "Come on, dude, just play it cool. Calm down and we'll get you out of this." But you've got to keep in mind that Jason is slicker than a greased pig turned politician. He was like, "OK, y'all. I'm cool." The stripper put her arm around him and started walking him outside. The next thing you know, Jason is gone. He disappeared like a fart in a tornado or new rims at a Puff Daddy concert. It was pitch dark and he ran off into the woods. Now, keep in mind that there weren't any lights outside my parents' house. It was so dark that when we grew up, we were doing homework by the fireplace. We couldn't find him.

It was pitch-black, Jason was stoned drunk, and he still had the handcuffs on. We kept yelling to Jason that she was a stripper, but he didn't believe us because she wouldn't strip outside. She was worried we were filming her or something. We kept yelling, "Jason! She's a stripper!" And then you'd hear a voice from the woods: "No, she ain't no stripper. Y'all are lying. Y'all set me up!" He was more confused than a blind man at a silent movie. It took us about an hour to get him out of the woods.

When we finally got Jason back inside the house, she started stripping. Jason was still in his handcuffs. We were more excited than woodpeckers in a lumberyard. She took her shirt off and then she took off her pants. Then she turned around, picked up her things, and left. "My hour's up," she said while walking out the door. We were more confused than atheists at a tent revival and hotter than forty acres of burning stumps, but that's one night none of us will ever forget.

You know, I learned a valuable lesson that night: Whoever said you can't buy happiness must have been dead broke.

[Things I've Found to Be True]

1. Brain cells come and go, but fat cells live forever.

2. If at first you don't succeed, destroy all the evidence that you even tried.

3. Junk is something you throw away three weeks before you need it.

4. If everything seems to be going well, you have obviously overlooked something.

5. By the time you can make ends meet, they move the ends.

6. If it weren't for the last minute, nothing in this world would ever get done.

7. Experience is something you don't get until just after you need it.

8. No one is paying attention until you make a mistake.

9. Whatever hits the fan will not be evenly distributed.

10. The most powerful force in the universe is gossip.

11. Everyone seems normal until you get to know them.

12. He who dies with the most toys is nonetheless dead.

13. Opportunities always look bigger going than coming.

14. Even if you're on the right track, you'll get run over if you just sit there.

15. Hard work pays off in the future; laziness pays off now.

16. In just two days, tomorrow will be yesterday.

17. He who laughs last thinks the slowest.

18. A clear conscience is usually the sign of a bad memory.

19. No matter what happens, someone will find a way to take it too seriously.

20. The hardness of the butter is proportional to the softness of the bread.

21. The colder the X-ray table, the longer your body is required to be on it.

22. Don't take life too seriously; you won't get out alive.

23. Anything good in life is usually illegal, immoral, or fattening.

24. The only way to get rid of a temptation is to yield to it.

25. A good time to keep your mouth shut is when you're in deep water.

9

Don't Ever Mess with Nuthin' . . . That Ain't Messin' with You

One of my favorite things to do when I was growing up was to go hunting. I used to spend the summer picking tobacco leaves, hotter than a devil's henchman caught in a wildfire, and dreaming of the upcoming days I could spend in the woods or the fields slinging bullets and arrows.

The week before deer season, I never could sleep. Most kids dreamed about bikes and games and girls; all I could see when I closed my eyes was racks and rubs, which made me happier than a fat puppy chasing a parked car. We might never have had much money, but we always had a freezer full of meat. Heck, I think we could have given it to Burger King their way, right away, anytime they ran low. If it flew, crawled, swam, or ran, we put bullets in it and spent many a night by the campfire swapping tall tales and remembering the one that got away. Fact is, every time I told my stories, the deer's rack would grow quicker than Pinocchio's nose at a women's Weight Watchers meeting.

Of course, my passion for hunting grew—and with it, the desire to hunt different game and see different states became an obsession to me. I'd save most every dollar I made, and planned to one day go on a trip and take my pops, since he had spent so many days in the stand with me—days when I made more noise than a blind billy goat with bells on his horns at a Sunday-morning service. We'd leave with nothing but dreams of tomorrow. I had decided that one day I was taking him to the place of no return for a country boy from the deep and dirty South: We was going north. Way north. So far up there you couldn't find grits or cornbread.

So I started looking around. When you work the fields and grow up on a dirt road, there ain't much you can afford. And I was tight with my money, too—tighter than a bull's butt on fight night. But I found this ol' boy way up in Maine that offered backcountry bear hunting; I figured this ol' boy right here might just have the setup we was looking for. So I booked a bear-hunting trip just a few miles from the Canadian border. The ad said they had all the amenities of the backwoods and would provide a real hunting and outdoors-in-the-wild experience. I talked ol' Pops into going—which was hard to do, 'cause he's funny about leaving the area around the house. But with enough persuasion (in the form of a fresh batch of his 'shine), I got him loaded up and away we went.

Now, I didn't know that Maine was basically on another continent. Heck, it took us more than twenty-four hours to drive there—and that was without taking any breaks. So by the time we pulled up, I was ready to pull my hair out. In fact, I would have rather driven a gasoline truck through a forest fire with a leaky valve. And if I had to hear any more of Pops's stories, I swore I was gonna swallow my tongue and beg it to beat my guts out.

When we did get there, I was more excited than a fat baby looking at a chocolate cake. We turned into a driveway that was seven miles long. Now, I'm from the cut and lived my whole life in the Lick—where snails are gag gifts, not hors d'oeuvres. But going down this path worried me just a little. We came to a little shack in the middle of the forest, and this guy came out to meet us. He was a big ol' mountain man, and as soon as he spoke, I just knew that by the way his breath smelled he had to have just chewed the butthole out of a skunk. Then some girl came out behind him that was ugly enough to stop a bucket of calf slobber in midair. But I must say, they was some of the nicest people I had ever met—at least, I'm pretty sure they was people. They showed us around the place and we hit it off like birdshot in a baited field. The guy took me to a hole with four two-by-fours in a square around it and a bucket of sulfur, and he said, "This is our outhouse." Now, like I said, I'm country, but at least we have walls on our outhouses so you don't have to worry about the neighbors (or the fire ants) getting too nosy! Well, I just figured there were plenty of woods around, so we'd make do.

Next we walked over to this long hose attached to a pump handle. I followed the hose and it ran straight down to the stream. Mountain Man said, "This here is our shower." I pumped that handle twice and the water that hit me was colder than a witch's breast in a brass bra in the Arctic. I knew right then and there that a blind hog had a better chance of finding his shadow than I did of using that thing.

Our next stop was the sleeping quarters, which was a makeshift bunkhouse on a dirt floor. Now, I had spent the better part of my life roughing it, but I quickly realized that this was rougher than a cowboy's rear end after wiping with 20-grit on the dusty trail. I also knew that if we were this deep in the woods and didn't find a bear, he was sure to find us! That made me happier than a two-headed dog at a cat show.

Well, that night I was colder than an Eskimo's butt on an ice toilet at Christmas, and was never so glad to see the sun coming up. The guide told us that you only hunt bears in the evening. So in the morning we'd go and bait the stands and work the area, trying to see where the bears were moving. Now, I know there were days I probably could have failed my IQ test, but I didn't see any need to go messing around on the ground near a bunch of bears. But since Pops always told me to be like a banana and hang in there with the bunch when we're out of our element, I figured I'd tag along and at least see the countryside. But that guide had a better chance of nailing wet Jell-O to an oak tree than he did of getting me on the ground at a bait site.

As soon as we started out, I was pretty sure this fellow was riding a gravy train on biscuit wheels, 'cause we jumped into a four-door 2500 series Dodge truck and he hollered, "Let's go to town!" Now, again, I'm no bear-hunting expert, but I was pretty sure the bait sites wouldn't be on the main drag. So when he pulled into a Hardee's forty-five miles away, in a town so small that the stoplight was a piece of colored construction paper that was green on one side and red on the other and directed by the wind, I was sure this guy must have been so dumb the only reason he got out of third grade was his momma gave him a crowbar.

He pulled up to the back of the restaurant by the grease vats—them great big ones that always sit by the Dumpster—and started filling up five-gallon buckets full of grease. Me and Pops just sat there in wonderment. But things really started getting interesting when he pulled up to a local doughnut shop and started rolling fifty-five-gallon barrels of old doughnuts up to the truck. He yelled, "Hey, do you mind getting out and helping me load these?"

I eased out of my seat, slightly apprehensive at what we were doing, knowing I wasn't gonna go to some Podunk jail for heisting larger-than-life Cheerios. I finally broke down and said, "Bo, what in the world are we doing? Are we gonna bait bear or fetch our dinner?"

He just laughed and said, "Sonny, we're picking up the bait! We've gotta swing by the gas station and get the lobster leftovers and add them to the mix. Then we put all this together and set it at the sites. Them bears will be all over this mush like bees on a honey-dipped hamburger."

True to his word, we pulled into a gas station that had a little room where you could get Maine lobsters for four dollars apiece—they'd even steam 'em right there while you got your gas and stuff. First thing I did was jump on that like a beaver on a petrified tree, and I ate my fill of them red devils.

It was about then I decided that there was no way I was going in the woods with this cat. I was getting the impression he was crazier than a corn-fed 'coon on coke. We headed forty-five miles back into the cut and got to the first bait site. That's when those lobsters started getting to me a bit. I probably should've stopped at one, but we didn't have food like that down South (and I couldn't afford it if we did). I told Mountain Man and Pops I was feeling like I'd been drug through the mud and left on the fence to dry, and I was just gonna hang out in the truck and wait for them to come back. I could tell from the look in his eyes that Pops was hotter than a gasoline-dipped hen at a chicken roast, but I just grinned and settled in for a short nap.

They took the four-wheeler off the trailer behind us and headed out into the bush, telling me they'd be back in about an hour. So I laid back in the seat and dozed off. I guess probably thirty minutes had passed when I heard the durndest noise. It sounded like a cow had eaten Astroturf, got constipated, and was moaning. I got out of the truck and started worrying. I didn't know what sounds bears made, but if that was it, all the food in the back of the truck, and the fact that I was stuffed liked a Thanksgiving turkey and reeking of lobster, probably wasn't gonna fare too well for me. So I jumped out of the truck. The only thing I had with me was my skinning knife, but I figured if this was a bear and he wanted a meal, he'd better pack his lunch and put on some boots, 'cause this was gonna be an all-day, uphill battle.

The sound got closer. It was moving toward me. I got more nervous than a sugar-dipped pony on a hill of fire ants and settled in for the fight of my life. Just then, a head popped out of the trees . . . and then a body. I was squatted down at the front of the truck and that critter walked within five yards of me. But it wasn't a bear—it was a baby moose! And it was cuter than a new puppy with his first spot.

Now, every moose I had seen up until then had been in magazines. They all had huge horns and looked like they could roll over a dump truck with a sneeze. But this fellow was no more than 250 pounds and looked like a little calf. He stopped, looked my way, and our eyes met. That's when I had my first epiphany. I had always heard that an epiphany was a life-changing moment when everything becomes real clear, so I knew that I had just gotten the best idea I ever had. Looking back, if I had been any dumber, you'd have to tie a flag around my neck to keep the pigeons off. But I knew I was going to catch me a moose and raise him up; then, when he got to be world-class, I'd sell him to the highest bidder.

Since I was a football all-star and in great shape at the time, I knew that I'd have no problem overpowering this little rascal, tying up his feet, and waiting for Pops and the guide to come back so we could load him up. But two things never crossed my mind: the first being that it is highly illegal to keep a non-domesticated animal, and the second being it's also illegal to take him across state lines. But I set out after that thing running faster than an ugly girl's blind date. Then, just like I was playing Donkey Kong, I had that moose in a headlock. It took me about three shakes of a mutt's tail to figure out it was really the other way around: He had *me* in a headlock, and he was slinging me around like a naked stage diver at a KISS concert.

'Course, I would rather have been super-glued to a chimpanzee with a blowtorch in a room full of dynamite than to let go. I figured he'd tire down in just a minute. But the whole time, he was making this horrible howling sound that was curing my earlobes, so I knew I had to get him calmed down—and fast. I could just imagine me and this moose in the Lick, being the envy of the whole neighborhood: selling moose rides, moose antlers, moose pictures.

Then another thing crossed my mind—or rather, my path, as he was dragging me all around that little field where we were parked. That ol' moose suddenly came to an abrupt halt. And I kept going. I must have slid farther than Pete Rose after his gambling conviction. And when I stopped, facedown in a mud puddle, I heard that horrible moan again. Only this time it was right in front of me.

Figuring it was the baby moose again, I scrambled to get back up before he got away. That's when I came eye-to-eye with Momma Moose. Now, it never occurred to me that this little fellow of only 250 pounds was still a suckling, and that Momma Moose probably wasn't gonna take too lightly to me rodeoing her little man. I ain't gonna lie to you here: I was so scared I didn't know whether to run or go ahead and say my last prayers—'cause the only difference between a rut and a grave is the depth, and I was pretty well getting ready to get buried.

Then my adrenaline took over. I jumped up like Carl

Lewis at the Olympics and headed for the truck with this 1,000-pound behemoth dead on my tail. I knew she was doing all that moaning, but all I could hear just then was my mind screaming, *Run! Run! Ruuunn!*

I was outta there like a bolt of greased lightning, and I'm not ashamed to admit I was screaming at the top of my lungs for my pops—begging forgiveness (which always beats begging for permission); I knew he'd be mad, but he'd know what to do. I saw the truck just up ahead and took a quick look back. Momma Moose was all over my rear end like a termite at a sawdust plant. I dove like Barry Bonds on a Randy Johnson fastball—right through the open window of that truck!

When I hit the seat, I thought it was my momentum that made that thing rock like a cradle going over Niagara Falls; but when I looked out the window, I noticed Momma Moose had rammed the door and pushed it in a good foot. I was screaming—and she was backing up for another go at the door. I knew right then why my momma always told me to wear clean underwear. And just as that moose started up again, I heard a pistol going off: *Boom! Boom! Boom!* The guide and Pops were screaming and snorting like cracked-out pigs in a rutting contest. The moose must've understood every word they were saying, though, 'cause she started backing off until they finally got between the truck and her.

Pops got in the passenger seat while I scrambled to the backseat. The guide climbed in the driver's door and fired that puppy up. But that moose started right in again at the front of the truck! You'd have thought we were two bulls fighting over a hot cow. The guide slammed that truck in reverse and started slowly backing up. I couldn't believe it. "What are you doing? Run over that crazy thing!"

He said, "Buddy, you got a better chance of finding a diamond in a billy goat's butt than going head-to-head with her. This here's a territorial issue and we have to let her win."

So after about fifty yards, she stopped, and with the little calf in tow, turned to head back into the woods. Just before they entered, they both looked back at the same time, and I swear they were staring right at me. 'Course, there was no way I was getting back outta that truck.

The guide and Pops were beside themselves laughing when I told them about me and the baby moose. I figured they would be mad that I got the door bashed in on the truck; but the guide said, "Son, anyone who'd do something that dumb has to catch a break every now and then—so we'll let insurance handle it."

Needless to say, I still went hunting—and I took two bears with my bow. I didn't worry about bears again that week. But every time I heard a limb crack, I was on high moose alert. I just knew that Momma Moose was out there waiting for me.

When we got back home it was late at night, and Momma asked me to tell her about our trip. Pops just smiled when I said, "Momma, the only thing I'm gonna tell you is I learned a valuable lesson: Don't never mess with nuthin' that ain't messin' with you." And with that, I went on to bed.

[Threats]

1. I'll beat the brakes off of you.

2. I'll beat you so bad, you'll think you were ate by a lion and crapped off a cliff.

3. I'll slap you so hard, you'll starve to death before you quit sliding.

4. I'll stomp a mud hole in your tail and then walk it dry.

5. I'll be on you like a duck on a June bug.

6. I'll be on you like a sewing machine needle: hard, fast, and continuous.

7. I'll slap you so hard, you won't wake up till your clothes are back in style.

8. I'll be on you faster than a crackhead on his pipe.

9. I'll be on you quicker than a fat rat on a Cheeto.

10. I'll go through you like a Sherman tank through downtown Atlanta.

11. I'll be all over you like a bee on a honey-dipped hamburger.

12. I'll beat you like an Indian drum on a wedding night.

13. I'll beat you down like a blind gopher in soft dirt.

14. I'll pop you like a two-day-old pimple.

[Country]

1. Country as cornflakes and gooder than grits.

2. Country as a baked-bean sandwich.

3. Country as cornbread.

10

You Always Catch More Flies with Honey Than Vinegar . . .
If You Want to Catch Flies

It was my younger brother Jason's senior week, and we had made our way down to Myrtle Beach to do some celebrating. Now, Jason had always worked harder than a forty-dollar mule, and he was pretty thrifty with his savings; but when it came to common sense, he'd have to study to be a half-wit. Seeing also how, at times, we got along like two shaved rats in a wool sock, we decided to drive separately. Jason had bought himself a yellow '87 Corvette convertible and he was as proud of that car as a short-legged puppy with two peters. Now, me, having a neck as red as five miles of Georgia asphalt, I went down in my '69 Ford F-150 with a six-inch lift kit and a three-speed on the column. That old truck was like a moped: she sure was fun to ride, but you didn't want your friends to catch you on it.

So we got down to the beach along with our friend John and, per tradition, piled in the 'Vette and started cruising the strip. Now, the two-mile drive down the strip takes about an hour and is usually slower than a herd of turtles marching through molasses in January. But the scenery is always worth the wait: the girls down there look good enough to run a bulldog off the back of a meat wagon at lunchtime. Shoot—if I had swings like some of them on my back porch, I'd never leave the house!

Well, of course, we got hung up at an intersection with about twenty other guys itching to piss on a porcupine and call the dogs. They started mouthing off about Jason's

'Vette, saying he must be a daddy's boy, and that got him hotter than a goat's butt in a jalapeño pepper patch. Jason can have enough mouth for about five sets of teeth, so next thing you know he was out of the car and those boys were right on us. See, when it comes to the ability to think things through, I'd have to say that the closest Jason ever got to a 4.0 in school was his blood alcohol content. But when it comes to fighting, he's about as crazy as an outhouse horsefly.

So though it was thirteen on three, we were holding our own. Heck, I hit one boy so hard I thought he'd starve to death before he quit sliding. But just as I finished with that punch I looked over and saw a fellow bury a knife to the hilt in Jason's back and he went down like a sack of wet potatoes. John had also been split open with a bowie knife from ring finger to rib and was bleeding like a stuck pig on aspirin. I broke into a full run and jumped on the boy who had stabbed Jason. I was all over him like a one-armed paperhanger with jock itch.

Then the cops came. When it was all said and done, the three of us were in the emergency room. John had thirty-eight staples in his side. Jason had a hole in his back that I swear was so deep we could have tapped into it and found oil. And I had two bones sticking out of my hand which, unfortunately, were mine. So the ER doctor recommended I head back to Raleigh and see a specialist, since duct tape and superglue were not an option. Problem was, I couldn't drive my truck, since it was a three-speed. So I talked Jason into letting me take the 'Vette and he could follow me in my old beater.

We were tired, beat up, and in severe pain, and none of us was looking forward to the three-hour trek to Raleigh. We started heading out of town with me in the lead and

Jason on my tail in that old truck. I pulled up to a stop sign on the edge of town when suddenly my door swung open and something got in and shut the door. I wasn't sure at first who or what it was, but it came together rather quickly. It was what we call a barfly around here—a lady of the night—who, during daylight hours, looked like someone had set her face on fire and put it out with an ice pick. Now, I'm not just saying she was ruined, but I've seen boogers on the bathroom stall of the men's urinal with more appeal. She looked at me and smiled, and I could see both her teeth. "Want to have some fun?" she asked. "For twenty-five dollars I could get you grinning like a shark at a fish fest."

Now, I'm not one to ever turn down fun, but I think I'd rather have a knife fight with Freddy Kruger in a phone booth than to hook up with this lady. So I said, "Miss, I know what this looks like, but I'm just an ol' farmhand. My boss just bought this car and asked me to drive it back to check it out. I ain't got no money and even less time."

She said, "Well, where's your boss? If he can buy a 'Vette, he's surely got some extra money to have a good time."

Now, being the thoughtful, considerate, caring person I am, and figuring that she was rough enough to gag a maggot on a gut wagon, I said, "Ma'am he's actually right behind us in my truck, that ol' beater. What you need to do is just walk back there, get in on the passenger side, lock the door, and go to having that good time."

She got out of the 'Vette and slithered back to the old truck, with Jason looking up at me as confused as a turtle on the center stripe. All I could do was break down laughing. I saw the old girl crank in and lock the door, and then she was gone. Next thing I knew Jason was jumping around in that truck like a kangaroo on crack. He burst out the driver's door of that truck and started yelling, "Ronnie! What did you tell this girl? What did you tell her?" I could hear him screaming, "Ma'am I don't need no help—and I've had about enough fun for one week!"

I put that 'Vette in drive and, in the rearview mirror, I could see Jason running away from that girl faster than Superman after ten cups of coffee. For just a brief minute all my pain was gone. I chuckled as I headed up the interstate, thinking, *You always catch more flies with honey than you do with vinegar . . . if you want to catch flies, that is!*

[Useless]

1. He's about as much use as a prefab posthole.

2. I see the screw-up fairy has come to visit again.

3. You could screw up an anvil with a rubber mallet.

4. He's not a complete idiot; he does have some parts missing.

5. He couldn't pour piss out of a boot if the instructions were written on the heel.

6. He's so useless, if he had a third hand he'd need another back pocket to put it in.

7. You couldn't hit a bull's butt with a bass fiddle.

8. That boy's circling the drain.

9. That boy couldn't throw a wet blanket.

10. The best part of him rolled down his momma's leg.

11. That boy's so slow he couldn't catch a cold.

12. She's 'bout as useful as the southern end of a north-bound jackass.

13. She's like a Slinky: basically useless, but hours of fun to watch fall down the stairs.

14. You're a wingless duck on the water.

15. She's got two speeds: slow and broken.

16. He's a poster child for birth control.

17. Some people are only alive 'cause it's a sin to kill 'em.

18. If that was my kid, I'd kill 'em and tell God he ran away.

19. He's 'bout as useful as chicken crap on a pump handle.

20. He's 'bout as handy as a cow on crutches.

21. He's as useful as a screen door on a submarine.

22. He's as useful as a dog with no legs.

23. He's as useless as boobies on a boar.

24. He's as useless as a pogo stick in quicksand.

25. That's why you have to support bacteria: it's the only culture some people have.

[Poor]

1. He's as broke as the Ten Commandments.

2. We were so poor growing up, my brother and me used to have to ride double on our stick horse.

3. We were so poor growing up that our roaches could stand flat-footed and screw turkey vultures.

4. He ain't got a pot to piss in or a window to throw it out of.

5. We didn't have enough money between us to buy misery.

6. We didn't have enough money to have anything but a bad time.

[Naïve]

1. He's greener than gourd guts.

2. That boy's so green, he ain't even climbed the foothills yet.

11

Save Your Breath . . . You Might Need It to Blow Up Your Next Date

When I went away to college, I was pretty broke. In fact, many days I didn't have enough money to burn a wet mule. So when I came home for summer break, I got it in my head I was gonna work harder than a four-armed tobacco picker and save every dime so I could head back to college and enjoy the next few semesters.

My brother, Jason, owned a roofing company at the time, and even though it was his senior year of high school, he had always worked hard and had great ambition. So, having worked in that industry for many years, I asked him to sign me on.

Jason looked right at me and said I was just a mouse trying to be a rat. Now, me and Jason got along in the workforce like a tornado in a trailer park. When we hit heads, something was gonna get tore all to pieces. Being a good brother, I've always tried to see things from his point of view; I just never could get my head that far up my tail. But after many hours of debates and begging and having to sign my life away in blood, he agreed to let me run a crew.

At first I was as happy as a pig at an all-you-can-eat slop trough, but then lunchtime came on the first day and Jason started in on me because I didn't caulk the flashing around the chimney. With four other guys on the roof, he laid into me: "I know you're not as stupid as you look. No one can be that stupid."

Now, I got three speeds: On, Off, and You Oughtta Know Better. And Jason shoulda oughtta known better! We started arguing, and just before it came to blows, Jason said, "You can shut up or step down. Remember, you came to me looking for work."

I had to bite my tongue then because I really needed the work, so I just turned around and went to walk off. About that time something hit me in the back of the head harder than a cowpoke's prick in a calf's tail. I fell off the roof and hit the ground like a human beanbag. I looked up and saw Jason standing there with a boom, which is used to lift shingles to the roof, in his hand, and fire shot through every inch of my body. I got hotter than a June bride in a feather bed. Then Jason yelled down, "If you're gonna work for me, you're gonna learn to keep your mouth closed and your tail catching!"

Now, I knew I needed the money, so I swallowed my pride (along with a few teeth), went back up that ladder, and headed back to work. The rest of the summer, me and Jason were up and down like a hooker on Saturday night, but I didn't ever let it boil over, 'cause I didn't feel like getting boomed off another house—or out of a job.

As the summer neared an end, I tried to get in all the hours I could before I headed back to school. One Thursday afternoon we were roofing a two-story house, working the very top section together. Naturally, Jason was nailing shingles and I was his laborer, bringing him heavy stacks of shingles when he needed them. I'd have to go to the ground, toss two bundles of shingles over my shoulder, climb the first ladder, walk across the first level, climb the second ladder, then walk the shingles over to where Jason was nailing. Now, it was hotter that day than a two-dollar pistol at an all-night shootout, so I had nothing on but shorts; I'd left my shoes, socks, and shirt on the ground. I could see one of them ol' summer storms blowing in and I was actually hoping it would rain for a few minutes and cool everything off.

When I came across the roof to drop some shingles, Jason started in on me about not having a shirt and shoes on. I said, "Bo, we're roofers, not politicians—and nobody's home anyway!" Then, before I knew it, he was up and all over me like a fat tick on a dead dog. I had finally had enough. I told him where he could stick his job and I headed to the ladder to get to the ground and leave. The last thing I remember was Jason yelling at me to go to hell, and I yelled back that I couldn't 'cause they had a restraining order on me there.

I had just started down the ladder when the lights went out. When I came to, my vision was real blurry and all I could see were bright lights and this beautiful face over me. I was just about to reach out to touch it and ask the lady if I was in heaven, when my eyesight started coming back. This lady was so ugly that if her face were her fortune she'd get a tax rebate. So I just figured I must be in hell. Then I heard the sirens and the lady was saying, "Mr. Shirley? Can you hear me?"

I answered, "Does a one-legged duck swim in a circle?" I realized I was in an ambulance—my brother must have hit me again with something and knocked me off that roof. I tried to get up but couldn't move my leg, so I knew I was worse off than a blind rat in an outhouse maze. I asked her what my brother hit me with, and where he was. But about that time I smelled something burning like grease in the bottom of an oven.

"What's on fire?"

The lady replied, "Mr. Shirley, that's you. I need you to stay calm. You've been struck by lightning."

Seems when I stepped on that ladder, it wasn't Jason that hit me, but a right hook from God Himself. The jolt had blown all the ladders off the house and knocked me all the way to the ground; in the process, it had blown off all my fingernails and toenails and burned off my eyebrows, my mustache, and all the hair in my armpits! The lady in the ambulance also told me that when I hit the ground, I jumped up and started running around in circles like a top spinning for a wrecked doughnut train. She said I kept yelling, "I'm on fire! I'm on fire!" Then I ran over to the pool and jumped in. Well, apparently I hit my head and went unconscious, and then Jason dove off the top of the house into the pool to save me. He pulled me out, did CPR to revive me, and got the ambulance there.

I don't know what made Jason take that jump. He must've been suffering from halitosis of the intellect, but he saved my life. I had to go into surgery to fix my knee, which was more twisted than a box of fishhooks.

As I was lying in the hospital bed that night, my door opened and in came Jason, wheeling himself in a wheelchair. He had poured ketchup on his head and rubbed grease all over his face. Ol' Jason looked worse than a one-legged cat at the dog pound. I was lying in that bed, feeling worse than death with a hangover, and I chuckled, "What are you doing?"

Jason said, "I just wanted to make you laugh—and didn't want to leave you here by yourself."

We laughed and talked and he got me a mirror so I could see all the burns and stitches in my face. I have to admit: I looked like my face had caught fire and someone had beat it out with a bag of bent nickels.

We had a good talk that night. And when Jason got ready to leave, I knew I had to thank him and tell him I loved him—but we just never talked to each other like that. As he was heading out the door, I started trying to thank him, but my tongue kept tripping over my eyeteeth.

Jason just smiled and said, "I know, brother. I'd fight a tiger in the dark with a switch for you, too, but you ain't gotta say it. In fact, save your breath. You might need it to blow up your next date, looking like that."

And with that he closed the door.

[Insults]

1. If I wanted to hear a butthole, I'd fart.

2. If I want more lip from you, I'll peel it off my zipper.

3. If you sow your wild oats, I'm gonna pray for crop failure.

4. I've seen freaks like you before, but I had to pay admission.

5. I'm not being rude, you're being insignificant.

6. I do understand, I just don't care.

7. I don't know what you drank last night, but your breath smells like the bottom of a birdcage.

8. I hope you get the fleas of a thousand camels in your crotch and your arms are too short to scratch.

9. Life is really good. Why don't you go get one?

10. Last time I seen a mouth that big, it had a hook in it.

11. My imaginary friend says you have serious mental problems.

12. Someone ruined a perfectly good butthole by putting teeth in your mouth.

13. You don't need a makeover; you need to be run over.

14. Your momma should have hit you over the head at birth and sold the milk.

15. Your trailer park called and said they wanted their trash back.

16. You've gotten all up in the Kool-Aid and don't even know the flavor.

17. Bo, you make more noise than a blind fox in a henhouse.

18. One million sperm . . . and you were the fastest?

19. Go tell your momma. I'm sure she values your opinion.

20. I had your cake and fed it to my pet gorilla.

21. Take a long walk off a short pier.

22. It's destiny that we met—maybe as a punishment to me.

23. You're the reason a man has a middle finger.

24. If dumb was hair, you would never need to shave.

25. I've seen more appealing boogers on a bathroom stall.

[Easy]

1. She's like a hotel doorknob: Everyone seems to get a turn.

2. There's no *I* in "slut" . . . but there is a *U*.

3. Her jeans are so tight I could see Lincoln smiling on the penny in her back pocket.

4. The trouble with a milk cow is she never stays milked.

5. Easy as herdin' chickens.

6. Easier than sliding off a greasy loaf backward.

7. She let 'em ride her like a borrowed Corvette.

8. Up and down like a hooker on a Saturday night.

9. I do all I can . . . and the easy ones twice.

10. Easier than telling a pig to roll in the mud.

11. Easier than making a blind preacher cuss.

12

Being Big Don't Make You Bad . . . No More Than Being Born in an Oven Makes You a Biscuit

From the time I was eighteen until I was thirty-one, my best friend was a mountain of a man named Johnny. At the time of his death, Johnny stood six-foot-six, weighed 385 pounds, and had twenty-six-inch biceps. He held the "Fourth Strongest Man in the World" title, which he won at the Met-Rx World's Strongest Man Championship in 2002. Johnny and I lifted weights every day. He also helped me lead my wife, Amy, to a World Powerlifting Championship in 2002—and she still holds more than twenty state, national, and world records.

Me and Johnny were more beefed up than Brahma bulls on a twenty-four-hour IV feed of Pump-n-Grow. But there was one thing we were not, and that was cocky. In fact, we were the humblest big guys you'd ever meet. See, when we were in our early twenties, we thought we were tougher than two-dollar steaks, and prettier than any cow chewing her first cud. We liked to frequent the bars down on Hillsborough Street by North Carolina State on the weekends, because the bars there would always have penny drafts and girls who were hotter than a mess of collards on the back burner of a four-dollar stove.

Normally we pretty much just walked to the front of the line and got in free, 'cause around these parts, we were pretty well known. One night we rolled into a normal hotspot and started gettin' wilder than a peach orchard hog.

Now, everywhere we went we were always the biggest and the baddest and did about what we wanted. That night, John Boy got locked on a girl who was finer than mosquito hair split three ways—but a girl that hot comes with a price . . . and usually a lot of problems. I tried to tell Johnny that we oughtta move on to greener pastures, 'cause I was sure a filly that tight was bound to have a herd of horses with her. But Johnny was more stubborn than a harnessed mule and had to have whatever he set his sights on.

Well, it didn't take long; ol' Johnny talked smoother than a baby's behind after a waxing and about had this girl ready to head out with us. But just then I noticed the bar got kinda quiet. Then I got this real hot burning sensation on my neck, so I spun around figuring I was gonna have to set some fellow in his place. That's when I came face-to-face with the Tasmanian Devil's brother. This dude was breathing fire! He was a right stocky ol' boy too, and I could tell I was about to have my hands full. Just off to his left was a fellow about my height but about 340 pounds— didn't look like he'd ever missed his momma's dinner bell. Well, I dug in, 'cause Pops always told me the first punch usually wins the fight. I was about to go through that boy like a Sherman tank through downtown Atlanta.

Then I heard a bellow. Johnny had caught wind of what was about to go down and he stepped up. Now, when I say Johnny was big, I mean he was so big I'd seen his shadow win a fight before. John Boy looked down at this miniature Spartan in front of me and slapped him right in the chest.

"You ever been beat down so bad you were eye-to-eye with the ankle bracelet of a flat-footed pygmy?" he asked. Everybody in the bar busted out laughing.

It was about this time that Raleigh's finest rolled inside and got between us. I knew something was wrong when the cops put their backs to us and started talking to the other guys—almost like they were protecting me and Johnny. I heard one of them say, "Now, Bear, you know if you get in one more fight they'll suspend you from the team."

Then the cops turned to us and said, "How 'bout you fellas start going ahead and leaving? We'll keep these boys inside."

Of course, this made me and Johnny hotter than a deep-fried habanero in hell! We were bigger than these guys and tough enough to tear up a train track with a rubber mallet. But we knew better than to argue with the police. So we decided to head on outta there. On our way out, Johnny grabbed ol' boy's girl and stuck his tongue so far down her throat he must've tickled her belly button. She didn't resist none either. Then Johnny looked back at the feller I was nose-to-nose with and he winked.

We rolled out back, loaded into John Boy's black Chevy truck with the six-inch lift and thirty-five-inch tires, fired that baby up, and let the dual exhaust sing. I was digging on the radio looking for some Hank when the truck cut off. I looked over at Johnny, who was looking bewildered, and noticed the guy from inside the bar standing on the step rail on the driver's side with Johnny's keys in his hand.

In a deep voice, he bellowed, "Get on out, 'cause we about to finish this." The Pillsbury Doughboy stood right in tow behind him.

John Boy looked at me and asked, "Which one do you want?"—like we were in a supermarket picking out the steaks we were about to fire up on the grill. I told him I'd take Doughboy and leave him the light work. I figured that way he could finish quickly and enjoy me rolling this gravy-train-on-biscuit-wheels around the parking lot.

Well, it was only a matter of seconds before I realized

that I couldn't have melted myself down and poured myself on this big boy. I tell you what: Getting on that 340 pounds was a heck of a lot easier than getting back off! That ol' boy was beating me like an Indian drum on a wedding night. I started calling Johnny for help, but when I turned to see where he was, all I saw was his feet where his head shoulda been and his arms folded around like a pretzel while this other guy was pounding on his face like a prison crew on a pile of soft rocks.

I haven't ever been so happy to see flashing blue lights and hear sirens! For the first time ever, the police actually *helped* us. They broke up the fight and Johnny came and helped me off the ground. The two of us looked like two toads that had just been out in a hailstorm.

The cops came over and told us to leave and they'd forget this happened. I was glad to head out with all my teeth still intact. As we were climbing into Johnny's truck, I asked the cops who those boys were. He told us the doughboy was the starting nose guard for the state football team and the other one, who they called Bear, was the national collegiate heavyweight wrestling champion.

Well, I learned two things that night . . . besides humility. First, never lock horns with a man named after a forest animal. And second, being big don't make you bad no more than being born in an oven makes you a biscuit.

[Afraid]

1. That made my nuts draw up so tight, you couldn't hit 'em with knittin' needles.
2. I ain't never been scared of nothin' but spiders and dry counties.
3. Courage just means you're scared to death but you saddle up anyway.
4. It's not the flying that gets you, it's the landing.
5. Scared as a sinner in a cyclone.
6. Shaking like a toothless dog at a bear jamboree.

[Speed]

1. Slower than a herd of turtles marching through peanut butter.
2. Faster than a jackrabbit on moonshine.
3. Faster than green grass through a greased goose.
4. Slower than molasses going uphill in a January snowstorm.
5. Slower than a sloth in a peanut butter field.
6. Slower than turtles screwing in molasses.
7. As fast as green corn through an old maid.
8. Slower than a herd of turtles racing uphill through superglue.
9. Faster than a frog on a fly at a maggot farm.
10. On it faster than a hobo on a ham sandwich.
11. On it like Barry Bonds on a Randy Johnson fastball.
12. On it like a bobcat with climbing gear on a phone pole full of catnip.

[Ugly]

1. She's so ugly, she could run a buzzard off a gut barrel at lunchtime.

2. She's so ugly, she could make a train take a dirt road on a Sunday afternoon.

3. She's so ugly, they filmed *Gorillas in the Mist* in her shower.

4. She's so ugly, she'd scare the balls off a low-flying duck.

5. She's so ugly, she'd have to sneak up on water to take a bath.

6. She's so ugly, she could stop a bucket of calf slobber in midair.

7. She's uglier than three miles of Alabama mud.

8. She's uglier than a five-gallon bucket of buttholes.

9. Everybody has the right to be ugly, but you've abused yours.

10. If I had a dog that looked like you, I'd shave his butt and make him walk backward.

11. You couldn't melt yourself down and pour yourself on me.

12. You look like the dog I keep under my porch.

13. You got more chins than a Chinese phonebook.

14. That right there is three pounds of ugly in a two-pound sack.

15. He's so ugly, his momma had to get drunk to breastfeed him.

16. He's so ugly, he couldn't get laid at a whorehouse with a handful of hundreds.

17. He's uglier than a monkey's armpit after a snot bath.

18. He's so ugly that if he walked into a cornfield, the crows would bring back the corn they stole last year.

19. If her face was her fortune, she'd get a tax rebate.

13

Don't Ride a Horse . . . Till You've Checked Under His Saddle

One summer day Jason, Johnny, and I were walking the strip at Myrtle Beach (which is where we always went when we were broke). We knew we could find some chicks hotter than green socks on a billy goat and get them to let us crash at their hotel. All we ever needed was gas money and clean clothes and we could easily pull off a stint at the beach.

Well, I remember that when we got there this particular day it was so hot you could sweat 150 pounds of fat off a 125-pound hog. So we figured we'd better hurry up and find some gals who wanted to hang out, and talk them into heading to their hotel until the sun went down so we could cool off and get some free grub.

Jason was always the pretty boy. And even though he had Champagne taste and a beer wallet, he usually could talk us into a group of girls and get us set for a few nights' stay. Now, I've heard it said that nothing is impossible—and I agree, because we had been doing both for a few years. But on this particular day, we were making about as much progress as a pogo stick in quicksand. It was getting hotter, we were getting tired and sunburned, and naturally our patience was wearing pretty thin. Jason had always made these trips worth the ride, but that day he was striking out like a blind batter facing Nolan Ryan.

Well, we rounded the corner and there was this girl standing there by herself. She had long, flowing, silky black hair to the top of her waist, legs that looked like they ran all the way to Georgia, and a pair of booty shorts hugging her behind. Jason puffed up like a rooster at an all-you-can-handle chicken feast and walked on toward her. Me and Johnny just waited, knowing we had this one in the bag: she was alone and Jason was in rare form.

Jason walked up behind her and said, "Do you know what would look really good on you?" He paused for effect. "ME!" She didn't even flinch.

About ten seconds went by. Jason thought maybe she didn't hear him, so he said, "This isn't a beach; it must be heaven with fluorescent lighting and you're the chosen angel."

Before he got the last word out of his mouth, the girl started to turn around. Her black hair fanned out in the breeze, her long legs pirouetted, her shoulders glistened in the sun. It was like a movie in slow motion. Then I noticed her Adam's apple. This beautiful, sexy, long-legged, black-haired angel was a *dude!* To top it off, he must've had thirty facial piercings, and on the left side of his face was a full tattoo. This guy was so horrid that if he would have walked into a cornfield, the crows would've brought back the corn they stole last year.

Jason looked like the bear that had just got his head stuck in the hive. A deep voice bellowed, "Look, chump, I appreciate your compliments, but this rear has an Exit Only sign on it." With that, he turned and walked away.

Now, Jason, being a man's man, was more tore up than a pay toilet in a diarrhea ward over the idea of hitting on a dude. Of course, Johnny and I were in stitches, having watched Jason try to pick him up like a lost dollar. So not only had he just crossed the gender line, but he crossed the bender one too! We started singing the Oscar Mayer

Me and Jason with my first sooner, Lil Jo (sooner be this kinda dog than that)

Mom locked me and Pops in the stockades at Busch Gardens

Feeding pigeons at the capitol building in Raleigh

Me, Pops, and
Jason modeling our
Christmas hats

Me and Shane Murray
at Atlantic Beach

Catching some walleye
in North Dakota with the
KFYR radio guys

Pops—just not giving a damn

Me and Jason bar-hopping
back in the day

Packing a rat to give to
my pops for Christmas—
he hates rats!

Hunting in Maine: the bear that made Pope and Young status

My sister, Sandy, and me at Momma's house

Jason working on the roof of the very house where I was struck by lightning

Johnny Perry with Amy and me at our first powerlifting meet with our four first-place trophies

Me, Jason, and his wife, Wendy, at Myrtle Beach after I took a beating at the hands of six marines

Me and Jason during our party days when I was first dating Amy

Amy's first night bar-hopping with me and Jason

Me and Amy at our first full power meet

Johnny Perry at the 2002 Met-Rx World's Strongest Man competition in Kuala Lumpur, Malaysia, where he took fourth place

My first Vulcan snatch truck and Budro, the blue Neapolitan mastiff that Amy gave me

Jason after winning the
Masculine Misfits award
at the Lizard Lick Festival

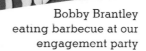

Bobby Brantley
eating barbecue at our
engagement party

Leaving our wedding on my Harley   Honeymooning in Aruba

Me and Alexa Rayne Shirley, my little girl, after getting her picture tattooed on my arm

Bobby, Brooks "Bubba" Ray, and Amy after a 24-hour shift

Amy and me when I officiated at the marriage of my tow manager, Brian

Preaching at a Power for Life team event

song: *"My bologna has a first name, it's O-S-C-A-R . . . "*
While we serenaded Jason, he got madder than a wet hen
in a Laundromat dryer, but we couldn't resist riding him
the whole rest of the day.

Well, needless to say, our chances of picking up a girl
that day were shot. Jason was so upset, he couldn't have
pounded sand into a rat hole. As we laid out on the beach
that night, listening to the waves crash and looking up at
the stars, we started planning our course of attack for the
next day. When Jason finally spoke he said, "I reckon Pops
was right when he used to tell us, 'Boys, God gave y'all two
heads, but He only gave you enough blood supply to run
one at a time.' "

Johnny looked over at him and answered, "If you'd
played your cards right, you could've had three heads
tonight—and a few stickers to boot!" Then Johnny and I
just started whistling the Oscar Mayer theme song again.

Jason threw us a few choice words and rolled over.
I heard him mumble, "I ain't ridin' no more horses till I
check under the saddle."

We all drifted off to sleep on the beach that night, but I
couldn't help but wonder, *What would Jason do if this story
ever got out?* I guess now we'll know!

[Dumb]

1. He's so dumb, he'd try to run the forty-yard dash in a thirty-yard barn.

2. He's a few bricks short of a wheelbarrow load.

3. He's not the sharpest tool in the woodshed.

4. He's a few sandwiches short of a picnic.

5. He's a doughnut short of a dozen.

6. He's so dumb, he tried to slap his reflection.

7. He's so dumb, he thought Johnny Cash was a pay toilet.

8. He's definitely nine dimes short of a dollar.

9. He's so dumb, he couldn't get into college with a crowbar.

10. He's so dumb, he couldn't hit water if he threw himself off a boat.

11. He's so dumb, they had to burn down the school to get him out of fifth grade.

12. He's as dumb as a barrel of spit . . . and half as useful.

13. He took an IQ test and the results came back negative.

14. If dumb was dirt, you'd cover 'bout half an acre.

15. If brains were dynamite, you couldn't blow your nose.

16. I know you're not as stupid as you look, 'cause no one could be.

17. I tried seeing things from your point of view, but I couldn't get my head that far up my tail.

18. The closest you've ever been to a 4.0 was your blood alcohol level.

14

Tighter Than a Frog's Butt . . .
And That's Watertight

One full moon–lit night in early spring, I didn't have any money, so I called up a lifelong buddy of mine and coaxed him and my brother into going frog gigging. Now, I ain't saying I'm the best frog gigger out there, but out of the six best in the country, three of them send me Christmas cards every year. I loaded up the johnboat and got my two homemade gigs, which consisted of two six-foot bamboo poles with small, three-pronged forks on the end. I grabbed a bottle of Pops's 'shine, and me and my brother went to get our friend.

Now, other than being a professional frog gigger around these country towns, I was the most hell anyone had raised in years; rumor had it I was so tough, I could eat gunpowder and fishing weights, wash it down with a Coke and a burrito, lay on my back, and cut one that could drop a deer from a hundred yards away. Fighting was all me and my brother were known for, and we could be meaner than a skillet full of rattlesnakes. So, as brothers do after about the third frog pond and half the bottle of 'shine, we started swapping "who's tougher" stories.

It just so happened that the Friday night before that, I had an altercation with a guy in a store. The guy jumped in his Camaro, rolled up the windows, and locked the door. Well, I had a gal with me who I fancied, so I was trying to impress her, and figured I'd punch the window and maybe hurt my hand and get some sympathy lovin'. I drew back and swung on that glass like Ken Griffey Jr. on a change-up and, to my amazement, the window shattered. I connected with ol' boy's jaw and he was out like a fat kid in dodgeball. I was happier than a possum eating fish steaks, but the girl wasn't impressed.

I knew this story made me the top dog of the night, but my brother wouldn't believe it. There I was, driving my five-speed Ford Ranger to the next frog hole with my friend in the middle between me and my brother, and he's telling me I'm lying like a rug in a dog kennel. Well, one kind word led to the next, and before you knew it, I locked the truck up in the middle of Jackass Road in Knightdale and we got out to do what brothers do best: test each other.

Jason was always a lot smaller than me, but he hasn't ever been scared of but two men: Pops and some other guy I ain't never seen. My brother's a sneaky little fellow too, and before I knew it he'd grabbed a frog gig and was slinging that mug in circles, screaming like a gladiator on crack and coming right at me. Every time he made a rotation, sparks would fly and the gig would make this crazy screech. I knew I'd better act fast.

I grabbed the other gig and held it by the steel end, and when he got in range, I just popped him with the bamboo end right in the mouth. Everything went silent. He dropped his gig. In the headlights of the truck I could see his lips swelling. Bo, the last time I had seen a mouth like that, it had a bit in it. He couldn't even talk. He just turned around and started walking off in the darkness.

Now my buddy started in on me: "You can't let him walk, Ronnie. Heck, if a car stopped they couldn't even understand him to give him a ride home 'cause his lips are so swollen NASA could orbit satellites around them."

Swallowing my pride, I got in the truck and eased down

the road, driving up right beside him. I tried to talk him into getting back in 'cause, to tell you the truth, we hadn't even hit the good ponds yet. The window in my Ranger would only roll down about four inches; I was yelling, "Get in!" and he was mumbling something that sounded like "Spew knew" while my buddy was laughing his tail off and swigging back the 'shine.

Just about the time we crested the hill, I'd had about enough and called my brother yeller. He stopped—and I could see the rage in his eyes. "Yeller" was one of the few words that would get him hotter than a hooker's doorknob on payday. All of a sudden his temper flared, his eyes went blank, and before I could say another word there was glass shattering all around me and blood pouring out my nose like a broken faucet. I had seen the punch coming, but I was frozen right there in the driver's seat.

I jumped out of the truck, ready to skin him like a Georgia catfish. We were nose-to-broke-nose when I heard yelling and laughing coming from the truck: "You busted the freaking winder!" I looked back over my shoulder and my brother looked around me, and we both realized at the same time that he had just punched the window out and broke my nose, all in the same swing. We looked at each other and just busted out laughing. Then we hugged, took a shot of 'shine, loaded back up, and headed out to the pond to finish the night.

On the way I told him, "Little brother, if I tell you the creek's gonna rise, you'd better get some waders. No matter what happens to us in life, we're brothers, and that means we're tight as a frog's butt . . . and that's watertight."

He just smiled. Then he reached into the truck, grabbed a piece of glass, and tossed it to me. Without saying a word I knew he had just one-upped me again.

[Cold]

1. Colder than a banker's heart.
2. Colder than an Eskimo's toilet seat.
3. Colder than a brass toilet seat on the dark side of the moon.
4. Colder than my mother-in-law's heart.
5. Colder than day-old penguin crap on Christmas Eve.
6. Cold enough to freeze the balls off a pool table.
7. Colder than an Eskimo fart in an ice storm.
8. Colder than a Colorado collie in an ice storm.

[Food]

1. That's too thick to plow and too thin to drink.
2. It's so good, your tongue will jump out and lick the eyebrows off your head.
3. That could gag a maggot in a gut barrel.
4. So good, my tongue is digging a hole to the top of my head and trying to slap my brain.
5. So good, it could bond a marriage back together.
6. That's like eating a TV dinner in the backseat of a car.
7. I'm so hungry, my stomach thinks my throat's been slit.
8. Ain't nothing salt and ketchup can't make edible.

[Hard]

1. Harder than Chinese arithmetic.
2. Harder than three-day-old snot on a hot oven door.
3. Harder to do than herding blind chickens.
4. Harder than nailing a raw egg to the wall.
5. Harder than pulling fly poop from a pepper shaker.
6. Harder than nailing Jell-O to an oak tree.

[Enterprising]

1. He could sell ketchup to a tomato farmer.
2. He could sell ice to Eskimos on Christmas Eve.
3. He could sell fish sticks to a crab-boat captain.
4. He could talk a stray dog into buying fleas.
5. He could pedal fire stock in hell and make a good living.
6. He could sell an angel a set of red horns.
7. He could talk a deaf man into buying a CD player.
8. He could sell thermal shoes to a legless man.

15

Either Fish or Cut Bait

It was the middle of summer and me, Jason, and Brian were about as bored as a beakless hen at an omelet breakfast. We didn't have enough money between us to buy misery, but we figured we could go quarter surfing till we got enough gas money for a ride to the beach. Now, if you haven't ever been quarter surfing, here's the way it goes: You call all your friends and see what they're doing, then you invite yourself over to their house. While there, you flop on the couches or chairs and dig like a miner snorting coal for some change. If you hit enough houses, you could come out with ten dollars or more—and we were the quarter-surfing champions. Heck, ol' Brian could pull a quarter through six feet of garden hose and come out with fifty cents!

So we made a few calls and ended up at the house of one of Jason's lady friends. (He had more women than Picasso had paint.) If you went to a girl's house, there was always money in the furniture because they were too scared to crack a nail digging around for it. It didn't take us long to scrape up enough to gas up and get to the beach. Of course, the lady was none too happy when she realized we just played her like an Alabama flat-top box—but that was Jason's problem. Me and Brian were thinking saltwater, sunshine, and small bikinis.

The day was so hot, the hens were laying boiled eggs. Since we didn't have much money, we figured we would swing by my grandpaw's house and see if he would give us some of his homemade 'shine. Now, Paw was partial to his 'shine and it was easier to steal the coins off a dead man's eyes than to get him to come off his elixir. But I also knew Paw took a nap every day at eleven and, if I was quick enough, I could sneak a bottle out of his cupboard. I also knew he had a string tied to the back of the door that was attached to tin cans. But if I slipped that off, I could sneak in and get the 'shine.

We parked down the road and walked by his living-room window. He was fast asleep on the couch. So we eased into the kitchen and slid the door open to the pantry. I undid the string and knew I was gonna grab that bottle and be outta there like a fat man at a New York marathon. Brian and Jason were as nervous as long-tailed cats in a room full of rocking chairs, but this wasn't my first 'shine swiping, and I had this plan laid out.

Well, as with most things I learned in life, I learned the hard way that there's more ways to choke a dog than to feed him peanut butter. It turns out Paw was ready for me. He had a big old rat trap hid up with the bottles and when I reached up to get one, that trap set down on me. You would have thought I was passing a kidney stone the size of a grapefruit when I let out my scream. Jason and Brian broke out; I turned around, and there was Paw with gun in hand, tears rolling from his eyes.

I begged, "Paw, please get it off! Please get it off!"

He looked me square in the eye: "Boy, if you're gonna try and steal my 'shine, you'd better be pretty slick—I can tell ya this is one test you ain't never gonna pass."

As he pried the trap from my now-broken fingers, he couldn't help but laugh. Then he turned around, walked over to the sink, reached under it, and pulled up an old mason jar. As he blew the dust off the top, he said, "I keep the good stuff in plain view, 'cause no one ever looks there. And since it seems as you're gonna be hurtin' for a few days, here's some pain remedy."

I was happier than a long-armed monkey with three peters. Paw said, "Y'all boys just stay outta trouble—and tell Jason I'll deal with him next time I see him."

I just gave him a hug and headed back to the car, smiling like a possum eating fresh peaches. Jason and Brian were waiting. Jason asked, "Did you get any?"

"Do rattlesnakes kiss gently?" I replied. I didn't have the heart to tell him.

Paw saw him, so I just handed him the jar. "Hit this and it will cure what ails ya."

Now, Paw's brandy was a lot like a garlic milkshake: smooth yet strong. So it didn't take too much to harelip the governor, and before we knew it, we were so tore back we couldn't pour piss out of a boot if the instructions were written on the heel. Somehow, we made it to the beach and headed for the water. We spent the rest of the day neck-deep in the ocean, slinging the bull and polishing off the brandy.

At dark, we decided it was about time to make like a cow turd and hit the trail. We didn't have any money for a room and there wasn't anywhere to go quarter surfing. Then me and Brian noticed a guy and girl laid up in the dunes making out. Well, I looked at Brian and said, "We can go home or get a free show. And my goer is skipping a little bit right now, so I say we stay for the fireworks." So, being typical guys, we eased up there on our bellies to get a bird's-eye view of the proceedings.

That ol' gal was hotter than a spayed mink, and that boy was just like a pet raccoon: his hands were on everything.

We were just lying there watching the show and had forgotten all about Jason, who was as tore up as a dollar whore on nickel night with a mattress for a backpack. Things were getting hotter than a billy goat with a blowtorch in a room full of dry cotton, when, all of a sudden, Brian started slapping my arm and pointing back at the beach. I turned just in time to see Jason, who had stripped down naked as a jaybird, running right at us.

Now, I have seen a lot of sights in my life, but I would have rather stared at the sun with a set of high-powered binoculars than see that coming at me. Me and Brian both figured he was about to launch himself on us. I started yelling, "Jason! You'd rather be superglued to a bar of soap on the shower floor of the men's prison than to sling that tallywacker on me!" Then, to my amazement, he went by us like we were chained to an oak tree, and sailed right onto the back of the boy we were watching.

He grabbed that boy's hips and starting riding him like a borrowed motorcycle. He apparently had seen that guy and was so drunk he thought it was Brian, and he was gonna have some fun with him. But Brian, who was laughing hysterically with me, started screaming, "Yeah, get it boy! That's how you ride a bull, Jason! Nail that to the ground like a legless duck in a dry pond!"

I reckon Jason thought he was rodeoing cattle. He held on a good eight seconds while that ol' boy was trying to sling him off. But Jason can be slicker than cat crap on linoleum, and since he thought he was riding Brian, he latched on even tighter and reached over and bit the guy on the ear.

Of course, that made the guy madder than a pig at a pork roast. Then Jason jumped up, laughing like a hyena on crack, and ran outta there quicker than green corn through an old maid. I've seen full moons before, but watching Jason head down that beach with a butt whiter than a bleached dogwood tree was better than a buttered biscuit to me.

Me and Brian were laughing like toady frogs on a helium high when that ol' boy jumped to his feet. His girl was laying there looking like she'd been cow kicked by a mule, and ol' boy was hotter than a four-balled tomcat. And I couldn't blame him none: after all, he had just been saddled and rode like a ten-year-old government mule. And on top of that, Jason had just ruined any chance that boy had of a romantic night.

I knew he was gonna try to run Jason down and beat the brakes off of him when he looked at me and Brian and asked, "Which way did he go?"

I tried to explain that it was just a case of mistaken identity, and that we were really sorry. But he rolled up on me like Hank Aaron on a fastball. That's when the tide turned. See, I don't fancy someone trying to bully me. I knew that Jason was in the wrong, but he was still my brother. I didn't really want to have to beat that ol' boy down like a blind gopher in soft dirt, so I said to him, "Bo, think about this for a second. You're gonna leave a girl that's hot enough to melt bronze in an ice storm here with the likes of us two rednecks just so you can chase a buck-naked man down the beach? That makes about as much sense as giving a monkey a math problem. See, this is one of those times in life where you either gotta fish or cut bait. So either get to fishing or get to cutting; but whichever you decide, just make sure you get to getting."

He stood there for about ten seconds looking like I might need to start watering him. Then he mumbled something under his breath and went back toward his girl. Well, I reckoned he liked the idea of fishing a whole lot better than being someone's bait mate, and he went right back to attending to his girl. Me and Brian went looking for the water-butt bandit and ended up catching up with him about a quarter-mile down the beach, trying to talk to a light pole and some sand crabs.

"Jason," I told him, "you need to learn to handle your 'shine or we're gonna cut you off in the future."

He just looked at me as confused as a mood ring on a bipolar chameleon in a Skittles bag. Then he looked at Brian and said, "Bo, I'm sorry about your ear; I hope your girlfriend's OK." Then he drifted on off to Drunk-too-much-ville.

I just smiled at Brian and said, "Well, if we wanna go fishing ourselves, looks like we already got the bait." And with that, I headed for the car.

[Pretension]

1. You're all in the mustard trying to catch up.

2. He's just a mouse trying to be a rat.

3. That boy's all hat and no cattle.

4. He's like a catfish: all mouth with little tail to back it up.

5. He's got a ten-gallon mouth and a five-gallon tail.

6. She's got Champagne taste buds and a beer pocketbook.

7. You're as fake as the handbag you're holding.

8. His alligator mouth overrides his Tweety Bird tail.

9. He's like a pissant with a hard-on, floating faceup on a leaf and tooting for the bridge to open up.

10. Where I come from, snails are gag gifts, not hors d'oeuvres.

16

If It's Got Tires or Testicles . . . It's Gonna Give You Trouble

In my midtwenties I got invited by the radio station KFYR 550 in North Dakota to spend a week hobnobbing with the likes of them disc jockeys and stuff. Now, I figured I was slicker than grease falling out of a barbecue biscuit, and I saw a week's free vacation, so I took 'em up on their offer. It was the most memorable trip I've ever taken.

I got to spend every morning broadcasting on the radio, every afternoon meeting the great people of the towns around there, and every evening hunting deer and pheasant. And then, after dark, I'd get more screwed up than a porcupine in a crate of packing peanuts. One night we even camouflaged a Ford LTD and hooked the windshield wiper lines back into the intake and filled it with transmission fluid, so when you hit the Wash button you couldn't see far enough to know whether to wind your watch or scratch your butt. The best part was that everything was all free, so I figured I'd take in as much as they were willing to offer.

In the middle of the week, I was sitting at a bar called Beers and Gears throwing darts and tossing back Red Eyes, when the owner said, "Hey, they're having a beer festival tomorrow night in the next town over and you can sample all night for free." Well, I was all over that like a sewing machine needle: hard, fast, and continuous.

Just after dark, I rolled up to the bar and we headed out. I'll tell you: it was more crowded than nine miles of

Alabama asphalt on Talladega Sunday, but we finally made our way to the tents. Everyone wanted me to sample their brews and try their dishes—and I just didn't have the heart to turn down such hospitality.

So before I know it, I had this guy telling me he had the best oysters in the state, and they were just picked that day and shipped in. Now, in my home state of North Carolina, there's two things we take pride in besides our dogs and our guns, and that's our barbecue and our oyster roast. I was trying to figure out how they shipped them on the same day! But Pops always told me, "If someone wants to give you something, take it. If you don't like it, you can always put it in the yard sale next week." So I stepped on up and got me a whole plate of them deep-fried jewels.

These oysters were a lot smaller than the ones back home, and sliced really thin—but I just figured that was probably a different way of cooking them. So I started putting them away like a crack-house rat on Cheetos. I have to say, after eating about twenty of them, I was really impressed, and smiling ear-to-ear like a baked possum. What could be better than free beer, free food, free transportation, and a free hotel room?

About that time, Disc Jockey Phil came over and asked me how I liked them mountain oysters. I just looked at him kind of cross-eyed, 'cause I hadn't ever heard of freshwater seafood. So with the intelligence of the southern end of a north-bound jackass, I asked him, "How in the world do you get oysters out of a mountain? That guy told me he had them shipped in today, fresh."

Phil busted out laughing. "They are fresh. We just cut them ones you're eating off Milton today."

I tried really hard to finish swallowing the gunk in my mouth. I knew I didn't want to hear any more. But before

I could walk away Phil added, "Those are *mountain* oysters—fresh off the bull!"

Well, the rest of the week I couldn't stop dry heaving. I don't think I said more than a hundred words over the next three days, and I assure you my body got as dehydrated as a dead pig left out in the sunshine. I now know to ask what's on the plate before partaking of the bounty, even if it is free. I just wished I'd understood Momma when she used to tell me, "If it's got tires or testicles, it's gonna give you trouble." Now I get it.

[About Ron]

1. I got three speeds: On, Off, and You Oughtta Know Better.

2. I was born at night . . . but it wasn't last night.

3. Sarcasm is just another free service I offer.

4. If I was any better, there would've been two of me.

5. I'm just like a banana: I hang with the bunch.

6. If you're gonna test me, this is one test you ain't gonna pass.

7. Bo, I'm busy just keeping it between the ditches.

8. That which doesn't kill me had better be able to outrun me.

9. I'm so bad I can make you put stuff back you didn't even steal.

10. Don't tell me you're depressed, 'cause I can always make it worse.

11. I don't suffer from stress. I'm a contagious carrier.

12. I live deep in the Lick, where sushi is still called "bait."

13. I've tried that yoga stuff but I think stress is less boring.

14. Sometimes I'm so great I'm jealous of myself.

15. If I can't see the bright side of life, I start polishing the dull side.

16. If I can't get what I want, I change my mind.

17. If I can't convince 'em, I'll confuse 'em.

18. The only thing I can't seem to resist is temptation.

19. I've never suffered from insanity. I've always enjoyed it.

17

It's Better to Let People Think You're an Idiot . . . Than to Open Your Mouth and Remove All Doubt

I was one of those kids who didn't have a lot, but knew it all. I believed, from day one, if I told you a mosquito could put out a forest fire, there wouldn't be any need to call backup in. If there was anything I didn't know, you'd rather be duct-taped to a polar bear waking up from hibernation than to try to teach me. Needless to say, I learned things the hard way: by running headfirst into many a brick wall. (Of course, it never hurts the bricks none; didn't even put a dent in 'em.) So when I married my first wife (and I use that term as lightly as I do "apple butter"), things weren't that different.

I was standing at the stairwell that led to the altar when my brother, who was my best man, opened the side door of the church. His '87 yellow Corvette convertible was sitting there, facing out and running. He said, "I've got a bag packed, a hotel room reserved at Myrtle Beach, a tank of gas, and a gallon of 'shine. Let's make like a baby and head on out of this mother."

I just smiled. "Jason, I can't do that. It wouldn't be right."

"Since when did you start doing the right thing?" he replied, and shut the door. "I'll leave her running, just in case. And remember: I love you, but I'm telling you, if you lie down with dogs, you're gonna get fleas."

I sure wish we would've cut outta there like a ponytail at an old-fashioned barber shop because I think the whole time I was married to that woman, she was still mad about that house falling on her sister in Munchkin Land. My brother was right about lying down with dogs; I *still* have the fleabites! Unfortunately, I was more stubborn than a corpse and didn't realize that getting on that train was gonna be a whole lot easier than getting off. Plus, the departure was gonna be twice as expensive as the original ticket. I did learn a valuable lesson from that, though: 100 percent of all divorces start with marriage. In spite of that considerable downside, though, I did get one great gift: my firstborn—whom I call Daddy's Little Angel. I thank God for allowing one of His angels to leave for just a little while— and for sending her to someone as undeserving as me. But you would've never known that at the time of her birth. See, like I said, I knew it all, and what I didn't know I could teach you. So when they came to me and said I needed to take Lamaze classes about childbirth and breathing, I told them they were as crazy as a crack-house rat in a flour factory. Women had been birthing babies for thousands of years with no problem. So when the time came, I figured me standing there saying, "Now, remember to breathe" would be about as useful as boobies on a boar. Besides, all my redneck buddies would think that I had turned soft— and I'd rather ride a tornado through an ape pen wearing banana underwear than lose my image.

So I skipped the nine months of Lamaze classes and figured I'd wing it; but the closer we got to the delivery date, the more nervous I got. When my wife finally said it was time to go to the hospital, I was more nervous than a Saturday-night hooker in the front row at a Sunday-morning church service.

We got to the hospital and I tried to act like I had it all to-gether. When we got into the delivery room and the nurse asked how I felt I said, "Just call me butter 'cause I'm on a roll." But the inside of my head felt like someone had slapped it around with the business end of a nine-iron, and my legs weren't none too stable neither. I felt like I was standing on a banana peel in the middle of an ice rink. To top it off, there was a severe thunderstorm outside. It was raining cats and dogs and, if you weren't careful, you'd step right in a poodle.

I had been struck by lightning and almost killed before, and that storm didn't make me any calmer. Plus, I couldn't figure out for the life of me why the nurse put my wife's head at the window end of the room instead of her feet. Here I was, a man's man, watching the birth of my first child, and I had turmoil in front of me, lightning streaking behind me, everyone screaming around me, and people yelling at me to "tell her to breathe and calm down!"

Trays full of tools were being wheeled around. Everybody was wearing a mask. And all of a sudden I realized that I was as confused as a tree-blinded possum! I didn't know whether to scratch my watch or wind my behind— but I sure wasn't gonna let anyone in that room know I was losing control.

A nurse said, "Mr. Shirley, do you know what you're supposed to be doing?" I said, "This isn't my first bull ride, lady. I'm on this like a pigeon on Big Ben. I got it covered."

'Course, what I was really thinking was that maybe I should have gone to some of those classes and at least learned the basics—but it was too late for that.

Next thing I knew, the baby's head was coming out. It was right then I knew I would have rather had a broke back in hell while pushing lava rocks than to be seeing what I was seeing! Now, you women know what goes on during a birth; but when us men have the birds-and-the-bees talk, we don't discuss the honey-and-scrambled-egg breakfast that accompanies childbirth. I was sure that this whole thing would run off me like water off a duck's back, so I just kept trying to act and talk like I had control of the situation.

I said, "It won't be long now! We're almost finished!" Well, my wife must've had a frog in her pocket, 'cause that's the only "we" that was almost done. I was just getting started. Before I knew it, the room was spinning like RuPaul at a Chippendale's show—and I got as sick as a green goose drinking gasoline.

No one in the room even broke stride. They kept yelling "Push!" and telling one another what to do. The machines were beeping, the lightning and thunder were banging away outside, and I felt like I'd swallowed a hornet's nest.

Someone kept asking me, "Are you OK? Do you need to sit down?"

"I got this, no sweat!"

Then the baby's entire head came out.

"Here she comes! What do you think, Daddy?" the doctor announced gleefully with a little chuckle.

Well, I looked down and all I saw was a blank face—no eyes, no nose, no mouth. And I fired up like a nitro car on a Friday-night drag strip. My eyes went blank. I got madder than a bag of wet hens in a hammer throw. I reached over and grabbed that doctor right by the throat, trying to pop his head off like a two-day-old pimple. I slammed him back up against the wall and I screamed, "You find humor in this?! My child has no face! She's blind. She'll never speak. What kind of daddy can I be?"

I was screaming at the top of my lungs and I could tell by the look in his eyes that he was as scared as a big-eyed toad in a hailstorm. Then I heard a baby cry. The nurse had jumped in and finished the delivery.

"Mr. Shirley, would you like to cut the cord?" she asked.

I let the doctor go and just stood there speechless. The whole room stared at me.

"How did she get a face?"

The doctor pushed me away and headed back to the baby. "Babies are usually born facedown," he said, looking at me like I was so dumb I would slap my own reflection. The nurses were probably all thinking that I was the kid whose parents probably just pissed in a boot and raised a blooming idiot.

"Am I correct in my assumption that you didn't take the classes on childbirth?" the doctor asked.

I just muttered, "Doc, is a pig's rump made of pork? I had no idea babies were born facedown!"

My new daughter was crying, I was crying, the nurses were laughing—and one even said, "Thank God she didn't breach and come out feet first. He probably would've thought she had extra toes on her head!"

I just smiled. There was this loud crash of thunder and a bright streak of lightning. I looked at that baby's perfect little face, her soft lips, her tiny fingers, and I began to sob all over again.

It was pouring outside and my emotions were raging inside. And I thought, Rayne—a ray of sunshine in a flood of emotions: that's what I'll name her. We called our baby girl Alexa Rayne.

I screamed out, *"Rayne! Rayne! Baby Rayne!"*

A nurse said, "Mr. Shirley, it's been doing that since we got in here ... and it doesn't look like it's gonna stop."

With that, I busted out laughing. Luckily, the doctor understood. He turned to me and asked, "Did you learn anything today during this life-changing experience?"

"I sure did, Doc," I replied without breaking stride. "Sometimes it's better to keep your mouth shut and let people think you're an idiot than to open it and remove all doubt."

With that, he smiled and walked away. I stood there holding my Rayne, and was never afraid of the storms or the lightning again, because now I had a reason to survive any rising waters.

[Mad]

1. Madder than Janet Reno's blind date.
2. Madder than a bobcat tied up in a piss fire.
3. Madder than a mule munchin' on bumblebees.
4. Madder than a pack of wild dogs on a three-legged cat.
5. Madder than a bulldog crapping rubber hammer handles.
6. Madder than a legless man at the IHOP.
7. Madder than a toothless dog in a meat house.
8. I'm mad enough to stump-whip chitlins with my head.
9. Someone peed in his cornflakes this morning.
10. Bo, that makes me so mad I wanna catch a Nolan Ryan fastball with my teeth.
11. She's just mad 'cause that house fell on her sister.
12. Madder than a wet hen at an omelet breakfast.
13. Madder than a pig at a pork roast.
14. Madder than a cowboy at a fashion show.

[Tough]

1. He's tough enough to stand flat-footed with a giraffe and slip it some tongue.
2. She's tougher than a two-dollar steak.
3. Being tall don't make you tough no more than being born in a garage makes you a BMW.
4. He's tough enough to chew up a ten-penny nail and spit out a barbed-wire fence.

18
Life's Always Simpler When You Plow Around the Stumps

Now, Sandy was always the baby of the family. We spent the first half of her life torturing her and the second half protecting her from guys like us. Most kids had little toy soldiers and maybe, at times, played with some sort of baby dolls; but in my house, you'd rather eat a razor-blade sandwich and drink a glass of saltwater than to be caught doing such a thing. So I decided that Sandy was like a life-size doll and a brother's job was to see how much we could get away with.

I remember the time when we wanted to play war but didn't have a hostage. So we tied up Sandy's arms and legs, duct-taped her mouth so she couldn't scream for Momma, and hid her under the shed as we set up our base. Well, there was two problems with doing things like this: First, you can't go to dinner and forget to bring your hostage! We had left her out there when that dinner bell rang. When Pops asked where she was, I got real starry eyed and mumbled, "I don't know." It didn't take me long to remember when he jacked me up like a Sunday-afternoon steak and told me not to piss on his back and tell him it's raining. So I led Pops and Momma to the secret base. That brought us to problem number two: I didn't know duct tape had a fondness for long hair. Worse yet, the glue on the tape had melted (due to the heat in the shed). When we tried to take it off, she was hollering like her face was on fire and we were trying to put it out with track shoes. Both

Pops and Momma were hotter than a shaved rat in a wool sock in the sauna. She lost most of her hair that day and Pops skinned me like a Texas turkey at Thanksgiving. But we won the battle and saved the hostage—of course, no one found any consolation in that.

Then there was the time we wanted to play war with bottle rockets but couldn't find enough guys to have a full firefight with. So me and Jason set up camp outside the back door of the house. We got some long metal rods and Jason taped a few bottle rockets together and loaded them in the back with the fuses hanging out. We were both smiling like blind possums in a persimmon patch, just waiting for Sandy to come out the back door. I knew this was one of my best-laid plans yet—this idea was so good it could bond a bad marriage back together. Well, what we didn't plan on was Sandy having friends over after school that day. So when the back door opened, we lit those fuses and figured we would send her running faster than a jackrabbit on moonshine. Just about the time them gals rounded the corner, the rockets took flight and I couldn't stop 'em. They looked like three bobcats caught in the middle of a forest fire with gasoline-dipped tails. Me and Jason went to rolling around laughing like two hyenas in a crack house— till we realized that Sandy's hair was on fire! (I don't know what it was about me and Sandy's hair.) I had set her entire head ablaze—and her friends' hair too! Well, they all went running for the swimming pool and jumped in. When they came up, they looked like they had dipped their heads in peanut butter and rolled 'em around the bottom of a birdcage. I knew when Pops got home, I had better go ahead and give my heart to Jesus, cause my butt was gonna be his! And he didn't let me down. He not only beat me like a burlap bag full of wet mice in a dryer, he got some clippers and let Sandy shave my head. (Now, you can imagine this big, tan redneck boy with a bright, white gourd that looked like someone had beat my skull with a softball bat. Needless to say, if I had a dog that looked like I did that day, I'd shave his butt and make him walk backward!)

Well, we went our whole lives back and forth, but you couldn't split a frog hair between me and Sandy when it came to brotherly love; we were tighter than the girdle of a Baptist minister's wife at an all-you-can-eat pancake breakfast.

I used to run her boyfriends off like stray dogs—didn't ever like any of 'em. Each time she'd bring a new one home, I'd tell him straightaway: "Everybody has the right to be ignorant, but when you started seeing my sister, you abused that right." Some of the boys she'd bring home were greener than gourd guts and pretty easy to scare; others were tougher than two-dollar steaks and took some working on. But in the end, I was always slicker than a minnow's pecker and found a way to run 'em off.

I don't know why she always brought home the types of guys she did. A few smelled worse than the outhouse door on a shrimp boat, and the rest were clueless. If dumb was dirt, they'd cover half an acre.

Now, Sandy brought many of these ol' boys over to see if she could rile me up—and a couple of 'em gave me a run for my money. But in the end, I'd teach 'em all that you'd rather eat a cold scab sandwich and a glass of snot than to cross me or date my sister.

Well finally, one day, she brought home this ol' boy who was more country than a baked-bean sandwich. He was a lanky fellow; as a matter of fact, he was so skinny his pajamas only had one stripe! And he was a tall ol' boy too: he stood about six-foot-seven. You could just tell he was a good guy. But I wasn't letting my guard down that easy. So when she introduced us, I told him to remember that getting on this train was a whole lot easier than getting off. He smiled and said, "Well, it's a good thing I don't like to ride trains."

So I said, "Don't think that 'cause you're a tall fella that I can't break you down. Bo, I am bad enough to uppercut a giraffe."

He smiled again and said, "Then I reckon I shouldn't ever go to the zoo with you!"

Well, I knew that this boy was slicker than the devil in velvet pants. When we got to talking, I found out he was a big-time hunter and he had more than four hundred acres of prime deer-slaying land. So I knew right then that me and him were gonna be tighter than Siamese ticks on a dead hound dog. His only downfall was that he was a little short north of the ears when it came to common sense. But his genuine good heart, the way he treated my sister, and the fact that he had those four hundred acres were good enough reasons to overlook it.

Now, like I said, I was very protective of my sister. So when I was at the house and got a phone call from ol' boy and he sounded like he was in tears, I figured he had gone and done something that I was gonna have to make him pay for. He sounded like he had shut his tongue in the door when he was trying to talk, and all I could understand was "It burns! It burns!"

I said, "Slow down, Bo. If you plant a tater you get a tater—and I can't help you plow if I don't know what we're farming."

He begged me to come over, so I jumped in my old truck and hightailed it over to his house. Now, the entire time, I was trying to keep in mind that this boy is so slow he couldn't catch a cold; but I was sure hoping he hadn't done anything to Sandy—otherwise I would be forced to make him as useful to society as a screen door on a submarine.

Well, when I pulled up, he was lying on the front porch in the fetal position, tears were streaming down his face, and he was holding his crotch area. Immediately, I thought, *Oh no! He's gone and done something he ought to have known better than to do and Sandy has John Bobbited li'l boy!* But I didn't see no blood, and he was still conscious. So I tried to ask him what was wrong.

He just said, "Please—get me to the hospital!"

I could tell he was circling the drain, so I loaded him up and headed into the city. He wasn't making any sense in his mumblings and I couldn't get it out of him where Sandy was. I kept trying to call her cell phone, but it was going straight to voice mail. The only thing I could make out was, "I'm dying! I'm dying!"

I said, "Bo, I don't know what you're dying of, but you'd better not get any over here on my side of the truck or I'll be on you like a termite on rotten wood!" He didn't even respond; he just kept wailing and stayed folded up all the way to the hospital—making more noise than a blind fox in a henhouse.

When we got to the ER, I carried his lanky tail in. That must've been a sight! I looked at all the people in the waiting room with their jaws open so far they needed Wide Load signs, and I said, "You'd rather have hemorrhoids the size of grapefruits than say somethin' to me right now!"

We got him into the trauma room and the doctor tried to rush me out. I said, "Doc, you got a better chance of selling ice to Eskimos outside on Christmas Eve than me leaving. If this ol' boy's got something contagious, I wanna know so I can get cured too!"

Well, they stripped him down and gave him a sedative. And when they pulled his boxers off, I felt like a dog choking on peanut butter. It looked like someone had set his entire crotch area on fire and put it out with an ice pick and a bag of fire ants. Up until then, I had never been scared of nothing but spiders and dry counties—but I was fear stricken at that sight! And I said, "Doc, I ain't got no dog in this fight, and I don't want none of that. And I need to go find my sister, 'cause whatever it is has probably done ate her up too." I grabbed the doc with concern in my eyes and said, "Is whatever that is catchable? I mean . . . am I gonna get infected too, Doc? Is my sister gonna be OK? She lives with this guy."

Meanwhile, the nurse was ordering tests and blood samples; she was talking about a flesh-eating disease and VDs and asking about his sex life. I said, "Whoa! Whoa! Whoa! He dates my sister. So if he ain't celibate I'm gonna be madder than a toothless dog in a meat house. You won't have to worry about the cure, 'cause that problem is fixing to be a lot worse."

He looked up and said, "Ronnie, you might want to leave the room so I can talk to the doctor. And see if you can get Sandy here."

I said, "Bo, you'd be better off shoving an umbrella up your tail and standing outside waiting for a hurricane than to say what I think you're gonna say. 'Cause even a dog knows the difference between being stepped on and kicked. The only person I'm calling is my momma." (Well, you know when a country boy breaks down and calls his momma, it's time to brace the doors, nail up the windows, and call the dogs in, 'cause it's on like Donkey Kong.)

He started screaming, "Don't you call your momma!"

I said, "I'm calling Momma!"

So there we were in the middle of the ER. He was buck-naked and his nether regions looked like a war zone for bull ants. Doctors and nurses running around in a frenzy, machines beeping, people looking around the curtains—and we were having an argument about me calling my momma. Just then, Sandy came running in with tears in her eyes and was yelling at me, "What did you do to him? What did you do to him?"

I said, "Baby, I just brought him here to the ER. He called me 'cause he couldn't get you, and he says *you* did that to him."

Well, that was about as subtle as an unflushed toilet. So then she was yelling at him. I was telling him I was gonna call Momma. He was crying and begging me not to. Meanwhile, he was trying to talk to Sandy.

Finally, the doctor yelled, "Wait a minute!" He looked at him and said, "Son, there is a white gel around your buttocks and down your leg. Have you got into anything?"

Still in pain, he said, "No, Doc. I took a shower and when I got out I just started burning. I looked down and this is what I saw."

The doctor asked, "Son, what did you use in the shower?"

"Just my normal shampoo. Oh—and I was out of body wash, so I used my girlfriend's."

But Sandy jumped in: "Honey, I don't use body wash; I use handmade soap. What did the bottle look like?"

He said it was a bluish-color bottle with white body wash that had a real funny smell. (At this point, I've gotta say, he was looking as confused as a monkey trying to do a math problem.) Sandy hit the floor, rolling in laughter while me and the doctors just stood there in wonderment.

Still in tears, the ol' boy asked, "What did I do that was so dang funny?" Sandy finally stopped laughing long enough to say, "Baby, you'll be just fine—trust me." And she whispered something in the doctor's ear.

The doctor just smiled and told the nurse to go get some gauze and burn cream.

I said, "OK, now that y'all got me more curious than a new puppy with two peters, let me in on what's goin' on here."

Sandy smiled and said, "I know that y'all think life is always easier when you plow around the stumps, but you have to make sure you're not riding in a barbed-wire harness! And if you're gonna use something on your body, read it before you apply! Nair apparently has some very adverse side effects."

I looked over at that ol' boy. "Now, don't that just dill your pickle? You used hair-removal cream for a body wash!"

He said, "I don't know about dilling it. To me it feels more like deep-fried!"

[Happy]

1. Happier than a possum eating persimmons.
2. Happier than a raccoon in the corn crib with the hounds tied up.
3. Happier than a possum eating fish steaks.
4. Happier than a puppy with two peters.
5. Happier than a punk in a pickle patch.
6. Happy as a June bug on a tomato plant.
7. Happy as a mule eating briars.
8. Happy as a fat puppy chasing a parked car.
9. Happy as a short-legged pony in a high field of oats.
10. Happy as a dead pig in the sunshine.
11. Happier than a horsefly trapped in an outhouse.
12. Happier than a hungry baby in a topless bar.
13. Happier than a two-legged dog at a cat show.
14. Happier than a starving bullfrog at a blow-fly convention.

[Fun]

1. More fun than a tornado in a trailer park.
2. 'Bout as much fun as skinny-dipping in a bucket of calf slobber.
3. I haven't had this much fun since pigs ate my brother.
4. Well, that was about as much fun as a nosebleed.
5. Laughing like a hyena at a pot-smoking convention.

19

You'd Rather French Kiss a Rattlesnake . . .

When I first started in the repossession business, things were much different from the way they are now. Back then, you had to work harder than a rented mule to get a car. There were no auto-loader wreckers, so we collected cars the old-fashioned way: usually on a rollback, which is a kind of flatbed trailer. Pops always told me to work smarter, not harder; but everything he ever learned I think he got from watching *Gilligan's Island.* Nevertheless, I talked to my buddy Brooks, and he agreed to help me nights doing repos. I figured the two of us working together would be smarter.

Now, when you repo on a rollback, you have to let the bed down, pull out the cable, crawl under the vehicle, hook it up, and then drag it on. So the process is about as slow as a herd of snails going through a field of peanut butter. Meanwhile, you're very exposed when you're doing all this. On one particular night we were searching for a Mazda Miata in a high-end neighborhood. Diving around there in that old beater rollback of mine, we were worse off than ducks sitting on the water on opening day of shotgun season. Every light in every house was flipping on, so I knew that me and Brooks were about to be in as good shape as a freshly screwed fox in a forest fire.

We rounded a bend in the road, and sitting right there in the driveway, shining like a five-carat diamond in a goat's butt, was our Miata. I told Brooks to run the VIN number on it as I backed up, and he was also to be the lookout while I crawled up under the car to hook the chains. Now, I've learned in this business (as in much of life) that it's always darkest before the dawn—so if you're gonna steal your neighbor's newspaper, that's the time to do it. And even though they could see us coming, with it being so late I'd have time to get hooked up before the debtor got out of bed and ran outside. In retrospect, I think I would have rather been superglued to a tornado in an Oklahoma pigpen than to have Brooks running blocker. Don't get me wrong: Brooks is a great guy. But in stress-filled situations he is about as useful as chicken crap on a pump handle.

After backing up, I jumped out and ran to the back of the rollback, grabbed the cable with the J-hook, and ran toward the Miata. About this time I heard Brooks yelling that someone was coming outside, so I knew I'd better get those hooks on. I yelled back to Brooks, "Keep him busy till I get hooked up!" After that, it's all hat and no cattle, 'cause there's nothing the debtor can do.

I slid up under that Miata and started hooking up when I saw a set of feet running backward behind me. It was Brooks, and he was yelling, "Stay away from me, mister! Don't swing that at me!"

There I was, under the car, possibly the worst position I could be in, and this guy had some sort of weapon—a bat or ax or shovel. I had no idea what it was, but before I had time to make a move I could see both his legs standing over me. So there I was, from the waist up under his car and him standing over me like a fat man at an all-you-can-eat pancake breakfast. I started yelling, "Brooks! Move this guy!"

But Brooks was about as useful as buttons on a dishrag. He just said, "Ronnie, I can't touch him."

"Brooks, you'd rather wear pork-chop panties and run through a lion's den than let this man stand here and whoop me."

Brooks didn't say another word. I could see his feet on the asphalt, but nothing was coming out of his mouth. Now, friendship can sometimes be kind of like peeing on yourself: everyone can see it, but only you get that warm fuzzy feeling. Right about now, however, I was questioning the limits of our bond.

I gritted my teeth and slid out from under the car figuring if the debtor had something in his hand, I could take out one of his knees and buy myself a few seconds. Well, when I slid out between his legs, I was face-to-face with what Brooks was so scared of. Only, it wasn't a stick, it was a snake—a one-eyed trouser snake! And that purple-headed creature looked like it was about to bite.

Now, don't get me wrong: The guy wasn't naked. He had some tighty whities on that had holes in them, and in his run to the car, his blue-veined doughnut holder had slithered out. So there I was, pinned to the ground, facing an irate man and his pet anaconda. I looked over at Brooks and saw that the reason he couldn't speak was because he was laughing so hard.

There are some days that I'm about as sharp as a cue ball, but it didn't take much sense to know that I was in a worse spot than a one-armed camel jockey with crabs. I said, "Mister, I'm telling you now: you would rather pole-vault over a barbed-wire fence with a rubber stick than to get any closer to me. If you'll step away and let me up, we can talk this out."

After a few seconds, he finally agreed to move over and let me up. The he flipped that monster up and put it back in its cave. I said, "Sir, I'm already hooked to your car, and after the mental anguish I just went through, I ain't letting it go."

Brooks was still laughing like a hyena at a pot-smoking convention while I was letting the guy get his stuff out of the Miata. I finished loading up the car, we climbed back in the rollback, and I was hotter than two rabbits banging in a gunnysack. Brooks had finally gotten back to the point where he could talk, so I lit into him: "Bo, you were supposed to delay the guy and block him from getting near me so I could hook up and get out. What happened?"

"Ronnie, wasn't nothin' I could do! He came out swingin' like a blind man at a prize fight, and I was havin' no part of that."

"Brooks, don't ever let that happen again. You've got to keep people off me. I'm telling you now: I'd rather French kiss a rattlesnake than to be put back in that position."

Brooks looked over at me and, with all seriousness, said, "Buddy, you just almost got your wish back there."

We didn't speak to each other the rest of the night.

[Dumber]

1. He suffers from halitosis of the intellect.

2. He's a few fries short of a Happy Meal.

3. He's a few clowns short of a circus.

4. His parents pissed in a pot and raised a blooming idiot.

5. You're like a genius . . . only different.

6. He'd have to study just to be a half-wit.

7. His front-porch light is burnt out.

8. If brains were dynamite, he couldn't blow his nose.

9. If brains were cotton, he couldn't Kotex a flea.

10. If brains were leather, he couldn't saddle a June bug.

11. That boy's dumber than a bucket of coal.

12. That boy's plum weak north of his ears.

13. That boy's so dumb, he could throw himself at the ground and miss.

14. That boy's so dumb, he couldn't cut a gopher from a wet hole.

15. That boy's so dumb, he couldn't pound sand down a rat hole.

16. Right there is a successful experiment in artificial stupidity.

17. There's proof that evolution can go in reverse.

18. The wheel's turnin' but the hamster's dead.

19. He never had both oars in the water.

20. She's so dumb, she thinks Grape-Nuts is a venereal disease.

21. She's so dumb, she thinks Peter Pan is a hospital utensil.

22. She's so dumb, she saw a truck full of Cheerios and thought they were doughnut seeds.

23. Her mind's like a steel trap: rusty and illegal in thirty-seven states.

24. His intellect is rivaled only by garden tools.

25. If she were any dumber, you'd have to water her.

26. If you put her brain in a matchbox, it would be like putting a BB in a boxcar.

27. The lights are on, but there ain't no tenants.

28. He got lost in thought . . . which must've been unfamiliar territory.

29. There was no chlorine in his gene pool.

30. She's as dumb as mud on a wood fence.

31. He's 'bout as sharp as a bowling ball.

32. She's as bright as a box of dirt.

33. He's as sharp as a bag full of wet mice.

34. She's as dumb as a cat trying to look pretty at a dog show.

35. If he'd been any dumber, you'd have to tie a flag around his neck to keep the pigeons off.

36. He couldn't engineer his way out of a paper bag with a box cutter.

20

There's Two Theories About Arguing with a Woman . . . And Neither One of Them Works

When Amy and I started dating, it was like locking two Brahma bulls together by the horns and throwing a hot cow in the pasture. Now, I was pretty fit, bench pressing in the mid-six-hundred-pound range and entering strongman contests with Johnny Perry. Johnny and I had been training Amy and she had just won her first world title in powerlifting—not to mention the fact that she is a redhead and that's like having a powder keg on the front burner of a five-dollar stove. Amy has also always been hotter than hell's basement on the day of reckoning but more ornery than a blind mule pulling a plow backward uphill. So naturally, it was only a matter of time before we would have our first throwdown; and I was determined that, when it was over, she'd rather stare at the sun with binoculars than to ever tangle with me again.

We were in Momma's driveway after an intense training session and we got into arguing over squatting techniques. Now, I'm not one who thinks he's always right; it's just that I'm never wrong! So the discussion got heated. Being of a somewhat more peaceful nature, Amy decided she was just going to leave and cool off. But when she told me that, I told her she'd rather slide down a mountain of razor blades naked into a pool of rubbing alcohol than to try to leave. Her ears started turning red and I could tell she was hotter than a baby's bottom after a spanking. She stomped over to her F-150 and fired that jewel up. I was standing about ten feet in front of the truck, thinking, *She won't run over me.*

That's when she leaned out the window and yelled, "Ronnie, you've got to the count of five to move." Then she started: "One, two . . ." and before she said "three" I was tearing my shirt off, telling her she knew better.

At that point, I don't know if it was the headlights coming on or the sound of the tires squealing that shocked me the most, but it was obvious my scaring tactics went over like a Little Person at a high-jump competition. Next thing I know, I was sprawled across the hood and she was flying down the driveway. I started begging her to stop. Then I knew I was in more trouble than a blind rat at the Cheesecake Factory, 'cause I saw her smile, hit the gas, and hook that truck hard right.

Then I knew exactly how Superman felt: it ain't the flying across the field that bothers you, it's the landing that'll cause you to kiss your grits. I looked up and there was Amy heading out of sight. I sprinted over to my Dodge truck and set after her like a duck chasing a June bug.

Amy didn't know this town too well, but I knew she was heading to the light by the Bojangles on the highway. I also knew she'd turn right and make her way back toward Wake Forest. So I took a dirt road, cut through at the Bojangles, and came the wrong way back down the highway. When I saw her turning toward me I dropped it down a gear and hit her head-on. By this time I was madder than Janet Reno's blind date. I ran to her window, which was down about six inches, grabbed it, and shattered it into a thousand pieces. Then I leaned in, put her truck in park, and yanked out her keys. I started screaming, "You'd rather catch a Nolan Ryan fastball with your teeth than just drive off and leave me like that! Now I got your keys and you ain't going nowhere!"

You'd think by now she'd be just a tad intimidated; but she was cooler than a Colorado collie in an Arctic ice storm. A few guys from Bojangles came running over, and I figured it was a good night to be heroic, so I turned my attention on them. Just as we were about to break out like inmates with a soap set of the guard's keys, I heard someone yelling. There was Amy, who, during the commotion, had gotten out of her truck and eased over to mine. I'd left my keys in the ignition when I jumped out, so Amy just backed my truck up, dropped that mug in drive, and was heading straight toward me! By the look on her face I could tell she was madder than a mule munchin' on bumblebees.

As I dove for my life, I'll never forget her yelling, "If you're gonna be stupid, you'd better be tough!" I lay there in the dirt and watched as she and my truck drifted off into the darkness.

It took two weeks, twenty dozen roses, and about twelve poems to get her back—and a whole lot more before she told me what she had done with my truck. But I learned a great lesson that night: there are two theories about arguing with a woman . . . and neither one of them works.

[Advice]

1. If you're gonna be stupid, you'd better be tough.

2. If you ain't got good manners, you'd better have fast reflexes.

3. If you think nobody cares, try missing a car payment.

4. When you hit rock bottom, you have two choices: climb out or dig.

5. Never argue with an idiot. He'll drag you down to his level and beat you with his experience.

6. Eat one live toad first thing in the morning and nothing worse will happen the rest of the day.

7. Never let the doorknob hit you where the good Lord split you.

8. Do your best, then just let the rough end drag.

9. It's always darkest before dawn. So if you're gonna steal the neighbor's paper, that's the time to do it.

10. Always forgive your enemies . . . but never forget their names.

11. Never go skinny-dipping with snapping turtles.

12. Never Nair your nether regions.

13. If you're gonna eat it, don't name it.

14. You can't fly with eagles when you run with turkeys.

15. If you're gonna talk behind my back, kiss my tail while you're there.

16. Remember: God gave you two heads, but only enough blood to run one at a time.

17. Never lock horns with a man named after a forest animal.

21

If Everything's Coming Your Way . . . You're in the Wrong Lane

Back in the day, when I had to haul a repo on a rollback flatbed, I found that taking the car was tougher than wrestling a tennis ball from an alligator. I could locate the collateral easy enough, but that was just the first step. Getting it hooked, loaded, and then driving away without losing a tooth was sometimes harder than Chinese arithmetic.

Then things were always made more difficult because my first agent, Brooks, had the tact of a Sherman tank in a china shop and must have learned to whisper at a sawmill—so we never had the advantage of stealth. Not to mention: we both had perfect twenty-five-year-old beer bellies, so it wasn't like we could hide very well.

One day our lien holder called and informed us that he had an unusually hard repo for us. The car was a Caddy with rims and the debtor was crazier than a hippie at a hula-hoop convention and meaner than a pack of wild dogs on a three-legged cat. Apparently, he had hired a repo agent before us and the car's debtor had beaten the brakes off of him. (And it didn't help at all that he was so little he'd have to run around twice just to make a shadow.) Well, me and Brooks figured this would be a good measuring stick for our talents, and it might even get us noticed by a few other lien holders (which would mean more business for us)—so we went for it.

Since this guy was well aware his Caddy was up for repo, we figured the best way to slap this bull was from the front. We were actually more excited than a Thanksgiving turkey in the yard the day after Christmas. So we loaded up in that old rollback and headed out like a herd of turtles.

Now, this debtor lived down a dirt path off a side road, and when you got to the end, his house was on the right and there was a neighbor's house just across the yard on the left. We knew that, heading down this path, they'd see us coming a mile away. And to tell you the truth, I'd rather have the fleas of a thousand camels in my crotch with my arms too short to scratch than to get spotted coming into a repo before I could get some chains on the unit. But in this case, we had to do the best we could do and let the rough end drag. Worst-case scenario, I figured, wasn't nuthin' a shot and a shotgun couldn't take care of.

Well, we rounded the corner and there was our Caddy. But I saw every light in the house coming on. I jumped out of the truck and, quicker than a fat rat on a Cheeto, I was under that car laying the J hooks on the axle. I crawled back out and started yelling at Brooks to tighten the cables. But as I spun around, I realized I was right about one thing: it definitely wasn't nuthin' a shot and shotgun couldn't handle! Problem was, I was on the business end of that shotgun and the guy holding it had crazy in his eyes.

"Mister," he said to me, "you're only alive because it's a sin to kill you. But out here, we don't worry about no laws. So you can either drop and run or you can stay and get dropped."

It didn't take me but a second to realize that I was ready to disappear like a set of twenty-four-inch gold rims at a Jay-Z concert. But since I had already hooked that Caddy, I figured I'd rather pound salt up my tail with a steel brush than to let that car go.

I looked him right in the eye. "Mister, before I can leave, I gotta get to my truck to loosen the winch and get these chains off." He agreed to let me get back in my truck, which was all the lead I needed to try and make an escape.

Now, this ol' boy might have been tough and crazy, but I quickly realized that he was also as dumb as mud on a wood fence. So I yelled to Brooks, who looked as confused as a pawless dog trying to bury a bone in an ice-covered river; I told him to climb in the car. The second his feet hit the floor, I sailed into that driver's seat faster than a jaguar on go juice and slapped that jewel into drive. I started dragging that Caddy down the driveway—with that man in tow— Brooks cheering me on like we was about to score the winning touchdown at the homecoming game, and me smiling like a catfish swimming upstream from the herd.

Dust was flying and the Caddy was bouncing around like a hobbyhorse at a birthday party. Suddenly, I saw lights coming toward us down the driveway. Seems his neighbor was coming home and we were hanging out there like a buzzard sitting on a gun barrel. At that point, I knew I'd rather skinny-dip in a pool full of armpits than to get back out and deal with this debtor—especially now that he had backup. But I was caught between the proverbial rock and a hard place. With nothing else left to do, I got out to face the music.

Well, like I said, the only thing we had going for us was the fact that this guy didn't have both oars in the water. If stupid could fly, he would have been a jumbo jet! But he was still holding all the cards—in the form of a 12-gauge persuasion tool! I crawled out with my tail tucked between my legs and just started unhooking the Caddy from the rollback. The neighbor had chimed in by this time, and it was really obvious that I was the bear caught with his hand in the hive.

But there's always more than one way to skin a catfish on a Friday night. And since this guy's neighbor was on the same intellectual level as he and Brooks were, I was in the perfect position. I looked over at Brooks and gave him a wink. Though sometimes he's as slow as a bucket of spit and half as useful, I knew that he was aware I was about to do something far less than stupid.

I've learned a cat will always blink when you hit it over the head with a sledgehammer. So I quietly said, "Sir, I'm really sorry we tried to pull a fast one over on you. If you'll give us the keys, we'll put your Caddy back in the spot where we found it and you won't never see us again."

Well, you could have buttered my butt and called me a biscuit when I saw him hand Brooks the keys—against the ranting of his neighbor. Brooks eased in and fired that Caddy up. I unhooked the chains and he eased the car back to the parking spot.

Then Brooks got out and handed the guy the keys! He was living proof that evolution can go backwards! Here I thought we were on the same page—but I guess Brooks was reading a different book. We got in the truck and, as the neighbor pulled his car around to let us drive by, I jumped on Brooks like a fly on a dead bull.

"Bo! What were you thinking? You had the keys! I bet your momma used to get drunk just so she could breast feed you and the buzz never left!"

Brooks never said a word. For the next ten minutes he let me ride him like a broken stallion, and I was getting hotter than a nine-inch rear end at the drag strip with no grease. Finally, we pulled into a store down the road a ways and I screamed, "I oughtta make you get your own ride home!

That repo was gonna put us on the map Bubba, and you blew it!"

He just started grinning like a mule in a watermelon patch and said, "I won't have to walk." Then he held up the ignition key for that Caddy. In all the turmoil, Brooks had slipped the key off before handing that ring back to the owner. "I couldn't drive off while the neighbor still had the driveway blocked, so I figured I'd think this one out, and I took the key. See, you're wrong sometimes, Ronnie. I do have moments where you don't need to water me."

I couldn't even talk, due to my ears connecting at the corner of my jaws. I spun that truck around faster than a frog on a fly in a maggot farm, and we headed back toward that Caddy. We parked about half a mile out and snuck down through the woods to the back of the house. Now it was time for some old-fashioned "Roncon"—the Lizard Lick version of recon. So we eased around the back of that place, trying to be slicker than a harpooned hippo in a banana tree, and saw that the Caddy was still sitting there, prettier than a Polish sausage at a pig roast. The lights and TV were on in the front room and the debtor was sitting in his recliner.

I told Brooks to ease over to the car, and when he got in it, to hit me on the two-way walkie and I'd bang the back door so the guy inside would run to the back of the house while Brooks fired that baby up. He had a straight getaway down the driveway, so it seemed like a perfect plan with everything in our favor: we had keys, we had the element of surprise, and we knew the layout of the land.

So Brooks eased around to the Caddy, and I went to the back door. Of course, we made more noise than a blind elephant in a china shop, so it was no surprise when I got into position that the back porch light came on and I was face-to-face with the business end of that double-barreled shotgun . . . again. I heard that walkie crack and Brooks said, "I'm in! I'm in!"

Before that man could spin Abe Lincoln's head around at a penny toss, Brooks fired that Caddy up. That ol' guy broke to the front of the house like Carl Lewis out of a cannon and forgot all about me. I heard Brooks mat the pedal and I could see a rooster tail of dirt all the way from the backyard. I knew we had just licked this repo—but I wasn't gonna sit around and gloat, 'cause I didn't want to meet the inner workings of those gun barrels.

I sneaked back into the woods and got a great viewing spot to see Brooks fly down the driveway with the man in tow. All of a sudden, I was as confused as a tailless cow during fly season. Brooks wasn't leaving the yard! He was doing donuts all over the man's flower bed! The guy was screaming and Brooks was giving that Caddy heck. I ain't never seen either of the Duke boys make a car talk like that! He went from doing donuts to making figure eights all over the yard—and from where I was sitting, it was better than Friday night at Talladega in turn four. I haven't laughed so hard and had so much fun since the pigs ate my brother.

Brooks was driving that thing like he was stealing it— which he actually was doing—and that debtor was getting hotter than a blistered pecker in a wool sock trapped in a sauna.

I was just amazed at how Brooks was holding that car in those tight turns around the yard and between all the trees. Finally, Brooks got her straightened out and headed down the driveway with the man running behind him screaming, "Stop!" (Of course, that man had about as much chance of Brooks doing that as he did of selling ketchup to a tomato farmer.)

Apparently, stopping turned out to be pretty good advice, because about halfway down the road I saw the lights come on and heard the brakes lock up. Brooks must have slid forty feet before stopping. There he was, in the middle of this guy's driveway, the guy running down the path behind him with a loaded shotgun, and he had the bright idea to stop! I was thinking right then and there that he was so stupid he thought Cheerios were doughnut seeds!

Now, I have intimidated and annoyed plenty of people when they upset me like this fellow did on our first attempt at repoing his car, but I have never been so bold as to take my chances when a shotgun was involved. I figured that Brooks was getting ready to get skinned like an Alabama river gar when I saw the door to the Caddy swing open. I knew then that Brooks was about to take a long walk off a short pier. So I broke into a full run across the yard to help him. I was about twenty yards closer to Brooks than the guy with the gun, and I started screaming, "Go, Brooks! Go-o-o!"

Brooks started screaming at me, "Get back, Ronnie! Get back!"

I couldn't for the life of me figure out why—till I saw a big ol' turtle head popping out the Caddy's door. Only problem was, it wasn't attached to a turtle. It was hooked on a big ol' Rottweiler! I could see the teeth and slobber everywhere. That ol' boy was barking and growling and biting at the air, and Brooks was pushing him out of the car.

I froze. Brooks got him out the door and matted the gas again, and I watched as he disappeared into the darkness. That's when I realized I was standing there with a rabid-looking dog and an owner with a shotgun! I figured you could just butter my butt and call me a biscuit about that time, 'cause I was getting ready to be done. But I broke back for the wood line as I heard that ol' guy screaming, "Sic 'em, Caesar! Kill 'em, boy!"

That dog lit after me like he was about to eat the tail end out of a rag doll. But I noticed he wasn't really gaining ground and I could hear him sneezing between barks. I got to that wood line and ran all the way back to the truck. Limbs slapped me in the face, briars ripped into my arms, and by the time I got into the truck I felt like I had just been eaten by lions and crapped over a cliff. I rolled out and called Brooks: "Meet me about two miles down the road at that little store!"

When he stepped out of the car, Brooks looked like he had been dipped in honey and thrown to the hornets. He was cut up, his shirt was ripped, blood was everywhere, one shoe was missing, and he was shaking like he'd just fallen out of a tree. That dog had been on him like a rubber-beaked woodpecker on a petrified tree.

"How'd you manage to drive like that with that dog all over you?" I asked.

"Drive?" he answered. "I wasn't drivin'! I was fightin' the dog! When I jumped in the car he was layin' down in the backseat and I didn't see him. About the time I cranked that Caddy, he was on me like a hungry bee on a sugar-dipped flower. When he jumped in the front seat, I couldn't get out; my foot hit the pedal and away we went! I never even touched the steerin' wheel until I finally got my can of mace out and sprayed him. After that, I couldn't see 'cause I sprayed myself, too! So I just grabbed onto the wheel with one hand and the back of his neck with the other and tried to hold on. When I could finally see again,

I got her straightened out and opened the door to let him out. Then I saw you runnin' toward us. But I had to swim or drown, so I figured you could fight him awhile.

"Ronnie, the whole time, the dog was drivin' more than I was." He added, "And just so you know, I'm done for the night."

"Brooks, I have never seen anyone drive like that! You looked like Richard Petty on crack."

"Bo," he said, "I felt like a Goodyear on the New Jersey Turnpike!"

We both laughed. Then we loaded that vehicle on the back of the rollback and headed for home. When we got in the cab Brooks said, "You know, I thought that was gonna be an easy one. We had everything planned out and it should have been slicker than summer snot on a doorknob."

I said, "Yeah, we should've known better. Like Pops always told me, 'Bubba, when everything is coming your way, you're either in the wrong lane or driving backwards.' "

[More Ronosophy]

1. Two can live as cheaply as one . . . if one don't eat.

2. There isn't any point in beating a dead horse. Of course, it can't hurt anything, either.

3. You can pick your friends, and you can pick your nose, but you can't wipe your friends on the seat.

4. Kind words aren't yelled.

5. If you lie down with dogs, you're gonna get up with fleas.

6. The best sermons in life are lived, not preached.

7. It never took a big person to carry a grudge.

8. Every path has a few puddles.

9. Every day is a roll of the dice, and some days you get snake eyes.

10. Even a stopped clock is right twice a day.

11. You can tell a man to go to hell . . . but making him do it is a whole nother matter.

12. If you wallow with pigs, expect to get up dirty and smelly.

13. If you can't race it or take it home to Momma, you don't have no business with it.

14. No matter how you clean a skunk, he's still gonna stink.

15. If a frog had wings, he wouldn't hit his tail when he jumped.

16. The early bird gets the worm . . . but the late bird never gets shot at.

17. The only difference between a rut and a grave is the depth.

22

Rapture Isn't What You Get When You Lift Something That's Too Heavy

The really cool thing about Amy is that not only is she as pretty as a possum eating persimmons in a pear tree, a world-champion power lifter, and a great mama, but she's also a licensed mortician. When Amy and I first started dating, we didn't have a lot of money. In fact, I had to fart to have any (s)cents in my pocket. But Amy was the perfect woman. She was so sweet, Willy Wonka wanted to sponsor her, but at the same time she was tougher than a woodpecker's lips dipped in cement. Most important, she loved me for what I had, which wasn't very much at the time, and that really hasn't changed much over the years.

I was so broke that whenever I drove by a cemetery and saw a freshly dug grave I'd have to stop. See, I wanted to give Amy things that would make her smile, and I knew how much she loved flowers. I also figured that since at times I was cheap enough to take the coins off a dead man's eyes, who's gonna miss a few flowers that would be rotten in a day or two anyway?

Hence, whenever I saw a freshly dug grave, I'd pull over and make outta there with an array of flowers like an Eskimo at an ice-eating contest. So whenever Amy and I went on a date, I'd show up with two- or three-dozen flowers for her. But the problem was that they were always short-stemmed flowers. When a florist makes a casket arrangement, he always cut off the stems. Amy would always ask me where the flowers came from, and I always told her

I bought them at Home Depot because they were priced half-off. Now, I ain't saying she believed me but sometimes Amy wasn't the brightest bulb in the pack—or at least, she never pushed the envelope!

But when Amy became a mortician and started spending a lot of time around dead people and caskets, she finally figured out that I was stealing flowers off graves. Bo, she was fit to be hog-tied and pigeon-toed! When I admitted it to her, she said I was about as useless as a one-armed mountain man trying to kayak across the Mississippi River.

Since Amy knew my secret, I asked her to let me start going to funerals with her. I explained to her that it was a great business opportunity and though money can't buy happiness, it sure can make misery fun. After a funeral, people always leave behind thousands of dollars' worth of flowers at the church and they never even make it to graveside. I didn't see why they should go to waste. I mean, those flowers could bring happiness to many folks and put a few dollars in my pocket. I could get flowers for my momma, or I could sell them on the side of the road.

Amy finally agreed to do it if I would give 50 percent of my earnings to the local old-folks' home. I love older folks anyway, and I knew she'd never figure out how much 50 percent of my earnings would be! I set up at the crossroads in Lizard Lick with about forty dozen flowers, and people could buy them for five or ten per dozen. Heck, after the first week I was high-stepping like a rooster with tube socks in deep mud.

One day, Amy called me and told me to come to the funeral home because she needed help moving a body. I went into the embalming room and she was standing next to a dead guy lying on a table. See, it was about this time that I should have realized that the fish rot from the head down. She ain't never called me before and asked me for help, but I was in love so I agreed to do it. Now, I don't like dead people. They're about as much fun as an inflatable dartboard.

I didn't like being around dead bodies, either. She knew I was as nervous as Rick James at a crack house. But when I started trying to back out, Amy started telling me about the process of embalming and preparing a body for burial. My stomach started turning, and I was feeling pretty light-headed. I didn't need Amy to tell me about draining a man's blood and releasing the gases in his body. I know I can get a good look at the T-bone by sticking my head up a bull's butt, but I'd rather take a butcher's word for it. I told Amy I'd heard enough and if she'd just shut her yapper I'd help and be done with it.

Amy was standing at the dead guy's feet. He was a very large man. He was so big that if he rolled over a dollar, he could make four quarters. Looking at his naked body, I could see why she needed help moving him. In all honesty, I had to laugh a little and told her there ain't no way I was standing at the feet. I didn't like the view. And when she chuckled, I knew I should've ran.

"Grab him by the head and help me lift him on the gurney," Amy told me.

I was about as uncomfortable as a hooker sitting in the front row of church. Amy picked up his feet, and I grabbed the back of his head—but nothing came with it! Now, right about then I knew I was more screwed than a Dallas Cowboys cheerleader after a twelve-pack in the locker room when the game was over. I looked down and saw that I was holding nothing but the man's head! I dropped it on the ground and blood started pouring out of the back of it. I was screaming like a dog wearing a shock collar for the first time peeing on an electric fence. Amy was rolling on the floor, laughing like a hyena at a Grateful Dead concert. The poor man had been decapitated and she had set me up like pins at a bowling alley.

Amy sewed the man's head back on to his body, and after I had emptied about four gallons of gut fluid and dry heaved for thirty minutes, I started thinking about them flowers and helped her get ready for the funeral. It was the first time Amy had been involved in a Catholic funeral. The man's family and friends were going to take communion during his funeral. I didn't know until after the funeral that if a Catholic priest blesses a bottle of wine, the bottle has to be drunk. See, if he blesses it, the wine becomes holy and then I reckon he's responsible for it. Heck, if I'd known that fact at twelve, I would've been a converted Catholic my whole life! If you bless four bottles of wine, and only one bottle gets consumed during communion, the priest has to drink the other three bottles. It's Catholic law. And the best part is, they use wine as real as Uma Thurman's breasts!

Before this funeral, the priest blessed five bottles of wine. Well, only about thirty people showed up for the man's funeral. I guess he was as popular as Godzilla in Tokyo, but all I was thinking was it was gonna be a slow day for flowers. Afterward, I was collecting the flowers to take back to Lizard Lick with me. I was happier than a mule in a briar patch. I guess all the folks who didn't show up sent flowers, and I had my truck as full as a sumo wrestler at an all-you-can-eat buffet. It was a Friday-morning funeral, and I knew I was going to make about four hundred dollars selling flowers because all of my buddies were going to buy flowers from me to take to their dates on Friday night. Where else could you buy a dozen roses for five bucks?

They were going to be on those flowers like Charlie Sheen on a high-end hooker.

We grew up going to church, of course, but I wasn't real keen on other religions outside of my own. In our church, when the pastor said, "I'd like to ask Bubba to help us take up the offering," five guys and four women would stand up. At my church, the opening day of deer season was recognized as an official church holiday. We always used grape juice for communion, unless someone snuck in a few drops of Boone's Farm.

After the man's Catholic funeral, I decided I was a little thirsty and took a swig of the communion wine. When I hit it, I was more confused than a blind man trying to open a revolving door. It was real wine! I started drinking more of the wine, and then the priest walked into the room.

"I have to drink four more bottles of wine," the priest told me.

"Well, I'd be more than happy to help you," I told him.

"No, you can't help me, son," the priest said. "I blessed the wine so I must drink it."

I scratched my head and told him, "Well, if you bless me and the wine's already blessed, then I can drink the wine. See, the way I see it is you got the power and I got the tolerance and we go together like Pamela Anderson and Botox, monsignor."

The priest blessed me and said a few ritual statements over me, and then we started in on the four bottles of wine. Now, I ain't saying I was having fun, but I felt like an invisible kid in a dodgeball game. We were on it like a harpooned hippo on a banana tree. The priest and I started having a shot contest right there in the back of the church. I went and got a Ping-Pong ball from the recreation room and we even played wine pong. I'd pop a glass and he'd hit the wine, and then he'd pop a glass and I'd hit the wine. Needless to say, after about an hour, we were more screwed up than high-top flip-flops. There wasn't a drop of wine left in the four bottles, but brother, I was surely blessed and felt rather angelic at the time.

But let's not forget that the priest still had to do a graveside service. The priest stood up and tried to walk, but he went about as straight as Boy George. He couldn't talk, either. He sounded like *Hooked on Phonics* in Japanese to me. We were just hammered.

Amy came back to the room, took one eye swipe at us, and said, "What have y'all done?"

"We haven't done nothing, I was just helping this priest out with his Catholic duties and felt the lead to do so," I told her.

She told me to take the priest to the graveside service while she cleaned up the back room and to mind my manners. She had no idea we were as messed up as a blind man trying to open a revolving door. The priest and I went out to the parking lot and he tried to get in the driver's seat of my truck, so we started having an argument about who was going to drive to the graveside service. Keep in mind that the cemetery was located just across the highway from the church, but we still had to drive over there. Neither of us could see the ditches, so there was no way to keep between them.

"Bo, I'm going to drive because you're drunk," I told him.

"No, Bo, I'm not drunk," the priest told me. "I'm just filled with the Spirit."

"Bo, let me assure you," I told him. "That's not the Spirit you're feeling right now—at least, not the Holy Spirit but maybe Boone's Farm spirit."

We didn't realize our argument was getting louder and louder by the minute, or that everyone in the parking lot was looking at us. The priest looked at me and condemned me to hell in front of everyone. I told him I'd been there, but was so mean they kicked me back out and if I could drink with a priest, I could fight with one too.

"Bo, I'm about to smack you so hard the picture on your driver's license is going to be swollen," I told him.

About that time, Amy and the owner of the funeral home came walking up. The priest was so mad, he was about to fight me. He really wanted to fight me! I told him it was a whole lot easier getting on this 250 pounds than getting off, but he told me he had God on his side.

I said, "Priest, I don't think God boxes."

The priest replied, "You never seen the Ali phantom punch?"

Well, it was on like Donkey Kong after that! He sailed on me, and I hip-checked him to the ground and then there came the funeral staff.

Amy broke us up and didn't say a word. I knew from the way she was looking at me I was as done as a Thanksgiving turkey at a chicken slaughterhouse. She snatched the keys and drove us to the graveside service. That priest was like a pine tree in a tornado during that service, swaying back and forth the whole time. I felt like a chimpanzee on a laced bunch of bananas. I was just as tore up as he was. I don't know what's in that wine, but that holy wine is some good stuff. I know when Jesus turned water into wine, that must have been a heck of a party!

The family was really upset. They were ranting and raving, and the priest was just trying to finish the service. I looked over at Amy and just saw rage in her eyes. I knew

I was in for it now. She was hotter than a mess of collard greens on the back burner of a four-dollar stove.

All of a sudden, Amy's face turned bright red and she started screaming. I thought at first I might need to say my last prayer 'cause she'd had enough. But then I looked down, and Amy's legs were covered in fire ants. It looked like she was wearing red socks. I'd heard of being hotter than a mess of fire ants in a flash flood, but this gave it a whole new perspective. She'd stepped right in a mound of fire ants and didn't know it! I dove toward Amy to get the fire ants off her legs, and I guess the priest had caught on too. He dove at about the same time to save her. When we reached Amy, we collided and bumped heads. Well, you know that went over like a trapdoor in a rowboat, and when I stood up, the priest was knocked out cold.

Amy just looked at me and said, "You're about as useful as a restrictor plate on a Yugo!"

I said, "Yep, but I am now blessed and the priest says I'm filled with the Spirits—or, at least a spirit."

She left me right there at the graveside madder than a toothless man eyeing a rib-eye steak. The man's family left because the priest couldn't finish the service. It was the most horrible thing I had ever been a part of. I might have lost my girl and definitely lost my best source of income. Man. I was as tore up as Noah with a woodpecker. I had to call Jason to come pick me up at the church. The priest was sitting with me and had an egg on his head about the size of a softball. It looked like he went headfirst into a bull. My arms were both swollen from the fire ants, and it looked like I had hemorrhoids the size of grapefruits growing out of them. I was just miserable.

The priest looked at me and said, "Well, there's only one thing to do at a time like this."

"What's that?" I asked him as I started to bow my head.

"Bless some more wine," he said.

I smiled and said, "Father, I like the way you think."

I finally learned that day that rapture isn't what you get when you lift something that's too heavy.

[Ronnie's Guide to Living]

1. Do not walk behind me, for I may not lead. Do not walk ahead of me, for I may not follow. Do not walk beside me, either. Just leave me the hell alone.

2. The quickest way to double your money is to fold it in half and put it back in your pocket.

3. The more you complain, the longer God makes you live.

4. Ham and eggs: a day's work for a chicken but a lifetime commitment for a pig.

5. Eagles may soar, but weasels don't get sucked into jet engines.

6. Don't worry too much about anything. Just do the best you can and let the rough end drag.

7. Don't sweat the petty things and don't pet the sweaty things.

8. I was thinking about how people seem to read the Bible a whole lot more as they get older. Then it dawned on me: they're cramming for their finals.

9. Borrow money from a pessimist; they don't ever expect to get it back.

10. When everything's coming your way, you're in the wrong lane and going the wrong way.

11. Duct tape is like The Force. It has a light side and a dark side, and it holds the universe together.

12. A conclusion is the place where you got tired of thinking.

13. You never really learn to swear until you learn to drive.

14. The problem with the gene pool is that there is no lifeguard.

15. The sooner you fall behind, the more time you'll have to catch up.

16. Love might be blind, but marriage is a real eye-opener.

17. Before you criticize someone, you should walk a mile in his shoes. That way, when you criticize him, you're a mile away and you have his shoes.

18. The main reason Santa is so jolly is that he knows where all the bad girls live.

19. Bills travel through the mall at twice the speed of checks.

20. Never underestimate the power of stupid people in large groups.

21. Sure you can trust the government. Just ask an Indian!

22. Conscience is what hurts when everything else feels good.

23. Love is grand. A divorce is about one hundred grand.

24. Some people are only alive because it is illegal to shoot them.

25. You don't stop laughing because you grow old. You grow old because you stopped laughing.

23

I Married Miss Right . . . I Just Didn't Know Her First Name Was "Always"

The day I married my Amy I was happier than Hugh Hefner in a sorority house. With all the bad I'd had in my life, I had spent many a year feeling lower than a mole's belly button on digging day. But for once, I felt luckier than a five-legged rabbit.

I had learned from my first marriage that you can turn a housewife into a whore but you'll never turn a whore into a housewife. So this time around, I was bound and determined to be more successful than an ice-water vendor in hell. I decided to ask Pops what the key to a long and happy marriage was. After deep, intense pondering for about five seconds, he said, "Son, you have to be the king of the castle. From day one, you have to love her unconditionally but let her know who makes the rules and sets the standards." Then he added, "Women are like tiles: if you lay 'em right the first time, you can walk all over 'em for life." So I started thinking of ways to lovingly let Amy know that things were going to have to be "my way or the highway" between us.

We had decided to get married on Halloween and have a costume wedding. All my groomsmen were knights with swords; Amy's bridesmaids were princesses; and we were the king and queen of Rontopia. All our guests wore costumes, and if you happened to drive by and see the festivities, you would have been as confused as a cross-eyed 'coon trying to cross the road.

Well, the wedding was a success and we had more fun on the honeymoon than a fat dog at a tire factory. When we returned home, I carried my bride across the threshold and remembered what Pops had said. I figured I'd better go ahead and lay down the foundation right away—but I also figured I'd have to be slicker about it than grease coming out of a barbecue biscuit. I set Amy down on our couch, walked into the bedroom, and came out with a pair of my pants in my hands. "Here, baby," I said, handing them to her. "Try these on." Amy looked at the pants and then looked at me as confused as a blind 'coon in a corn maze.

"Ronnie," she said, "you know these are too big for me. I can't wear them." Smiling from ear-to-ear, I replied, "That's right, honey, and you always remember that. You'll never be able to wear my pants in this house. As long as we both understand that, we'll be as happy as a mule munching on briars."

Amy just smiled and said, "OK."

I left that room stepping higher than a high-socked rooster in a pigpen. Well, a few hours flew by and we were getting ready for our first night in our house together as husband and wife. When I pulled the sheets down on the bed, there was a set of Amy's jeans lying on my pillow.

"Baby, why are these on my pillow?" I asked her.

She walked in the room and said, "Oh, I wanted you to try them on."

I just started laughing. "Amy, you know I can't get into your pants. I'd have a better chance of trying to nail Jell-O to an oak tree."

Amy just smiled. Then, as she got ready to turn out the light, she looked me in the eye and said, "That's right, honey. You can't get into my pants. And until you decide to let me wear yours, you're never gonna get into them again."

With that, she snapped off the light and I was surrounded by darkness. As I laid back on the bed, knowing that sleep was all I'd be getting that night, I realized two things: one, never take marital advice from a man who sleeps in his own room alone; and two, I had definitely married Miss Right. It just took me until that moment to realize her first name was "Always."

[Leaving]

1. Make like a cow turd and hit the trail.
2. Make like a baby and head outta this mother.
3. Make like a tree in the fall and leave.
4. Headed off like a herd of turtles.
5. Outta there like a fat kid in dodgeball.
6. I'll leave you behind like you were chained to an oak tree.
7. Outta there like a one-legged man at a breakdancing contest.
8. Outta there like a ponytail at an old-fashioned barber shop.
9. Outta there like a fat man at the New York Marathon.
10. Break out like inmates with a soap set of the guard's keys.
11. We're off like a prom dress.

[Lying]

1. As full of wind as a pig eating baked beans.
2. She's lying like a flat snake in tall grass.
3. It's your lie: tell it like you want to.
4. Don't piss on my back and tell me it's raining.
5. My cow died last night, so I don't need your bull today.
6. He's lying like a cheap rug in a Laundromat.

24

There Ain't No Sense in Beating a Dead Horse . . . 'Course, It Can't Hurt None Neither

One of the things I've dreaded most over the last few years is Saturday-morning breakfast at Momma's house. Now, don't get me wrong. Everyone knows her cooking is so good it could make your tongue jump out and lick the eyebrows off your head. And if she ever got to making them cat-head biscuits and molasses, my tongue would pure drill a hole in the roof of my mouth and slap my brain around till it told my mouth to take another bite. The problem was Amy.

See, she always pulled a double shift at the funeral home Friday night into Saturday, and that meant she had to pick up bodies at various places and transport them. She drove this big ol' spooky van that we referred to as the meat wagon. Normally, I'd rather have hemorrhoids the size of grapefruits than to be around when she showed up in that thing. As I mentioned earlier, I didn't take a liking to being around the deceased or anything that had to do with them; it just really always creeped me out. But if Amy had a call, she would always swing by Momma's in that meat wagon afterward, roll up inside like nothing was different, and sit down to breakfast with us.

Now, needless to say, every time this happened I was outta there like a one-legged man at a breakdancing contest. Amy always found it funny. And she knew if she called and told everyone she was on the way, then there would always be plenty of food—'cause once I got that info I'd feel sicker than Lady Gaga's blind date after the introduction.

My momma could slap-cook some country breakfasts, and it got to where Amy was ruining them almost every week. So I finally broke down and told Momma I was gonna fix Amy the next time she came by on a Saturday morning. I figured I'd leave like I normally did when she arrived; but instead of driving off, I'd park up the road, run back through the woods to Momma's house, and climb into the back of that meat wagon. I'd hang out there until Amy started down the road, then I'd jump out and scare her so bad her eyes would bug out like a toady frog in a hailstorm. I figured this might break her from the habit of coming over if I started messing with her every time she did. Problem was, I told Momma my plan in front of Jason.

You've gotta remember that Jason's sneaky enough, but when it comes to smarts, if brains were gas he wouldn't have enough to run an ant's go-kart halfway around a Cheerio. Now, Jason is the type of brother who is just like a billy goat—hardheaded with a stinkin' tail—so I should have known at some point he was gonna throw a kink into my plan.

Well, sure enough, the next Saturday rolled around and we were eating hot grits and link sausage with red-eye gravy when the phone rang. It was Amy and she was coming over. I will tell you I was happier than a starving bullfrog at a blow-fly convention. She rolled in, gave me a kiss, and asked me if I was staying and eating with her—with that smart smirk across her face that she does so well.

"If you believe I'm staying here with you and that van, you must think Grape-Nuts are a venereal disease and Peter Pan is a hospital utensil."

She just laughed as I kissed her good-bye. Then I made

like a baby and headed on outta there. I just couldn't wait to sneak back around and finally ruin one of *her* Saturday mornings! As luck would have it, she left the door unlocked. So I climbed in and then froze. I'd forgotten how horrified I was of this van in the first place! Once I got in, I realized this might not be the brightest idea I ever had. Then I remembered that Pops always told me courage was being scared to death but saddling up anyway, so I eased into the back.

I had never seen the inside of one of these things. There were two stretchers lying there: one on each side. Problem was, they both had these black body bags laid on them— but one was full and zipped all the way to the top. Now, I could tell that wasn't a bag of dirty laundry in there and I was more nervous than a three-legged cat trying to cover crap on an icy pond. I knew Amy never brought bodies over, but maybe this time she was in a hurry. I decided it wasn't gonna take me but an instant to get out of that van. But when I turned to head out I saw her coming out the door. I was trapped—I knew exactly how a long-tailed mountain lion feels in a room full of rat traps.

Well, I figured I could either man up or cut and run. But since I was this deep in the water, I figured I might as well finish swimming. I jumped into the other bag and zipped it almost to the top. There wasn't a zipper on the inside, so I knew I had to let my hand hang out of the hole so I could get it unzipped when it came time to climb out to scare Amy.

Man, that bag was hotter than two furry rats banging in a wool sock in a sauna; I was sweating like a pig at a hot-dog plant. I could hear Amy get in. She cranked up the van and then turned up the radio. This was great because it would cover any noise I made getting out of the bag. I felt the bumps as we went out of the driveway, and

I could feel the van turn to the right and pick up speed. Now, I had no idea that this ride would be as bumpy as the back of Fat Albert's head, but she nearly slung me off the stretcher three or four times. It was a good thing that the folks who usually rode in this wagon weren't alive, 'cause if they were she'd have killed 'em with her driving!

After a few minutes of being shaken worse than a pit bull crapping hatchet handles, I decided to spring into action and give her the scare of her life. I eased that zipper about halfway down. I could hear Amy singing along with the radio, so I knew she wasn't paying any attention to what was going on behind her. I slipped over to the side of the stretcher, just waiting until we got to a stoplight so she didn't wreck when I jumped out at her like a bucktoothed mule on a patch of briars.

Just as we began to ease up to a stoplight, I could see out the window that we were in front of a church—and the church was having a wedding. There were flowers all over and people standing around outside. I thought, *Man, I'm gonna scare her so bad she'll jump out and make a fool of herself in front of this whole wedding party. I bet she won't ever mess with our Saturday-morning breakfasts again!*

That's when I heard some moaning that seemed to be coming from the other bag. I figured I was just hearing some feedback from the rear speakers, 'cause there wasn't any way that a dead person would be making those sounds!

Or maybe the truck had a whine that sounded like a moan. But it kept getting louder and louder. It was at that moment I saw my life flash before my eyes.

I was as scared as a sinner in a cyclone and couldn't even speak. I wanted to call to Amy, but she was up there just looking at the light and singing—and I couldn't even mumble. That's when it happened. I would have rather been a short-legged rooster in a high-water hog pen than to see what I saw next: the bag started moving—like someone was trying to get out!

I knew I would rather be pecked to death by a crow with a rubber beak than to be in the back of that van at that moment. I looked around and saw this broom-shaped thing lying on the floor next to me. Then I did what any tough-as-nails feisty young redneck would do: I grabbed that thing and started screaming for Amy as I laid into the body bag like a fat boy on a chocolate cake.

I was screaming and swinging, and the moaning turned into yelling: "Stop! Stop it! Uhh! Ohh!"

The more it yelled, the harder I swung. I was on that bag and whatever was in it like a pack of cracked-out dogs on a three-legged cat. I was gonna make sure when I was done with whatever had come to life, it was as useless as a cow with crutches.

Next thing I knew, the back door swung open and Amy was snatching me out so fast I thought I was stuck hub-deep to a Ferris wheel. She was screaming for me to stop—and I was screaming for her to run.

"I don't know what it is, honey, but I'm gonna beat the brakes off of it!" Then I sailed back into the van and onto that bag like a bobcat with climbing gear on a phone pole full of catnip.

Amy jumped back in and lay across the body, which had stopped moving and groaning by then. I just looked at her and said, "Are you crazy? Move so I can kill it . . . again!"

She reached up and grabbed the zipper. That's when I screamed, "You'd rather be superglued to the Tasmanian Devil in a phone booth than to let that thing out!"

But she pulled the zipper to the bottom and slung the sides of the bag open. Now, about this time I realized that we were at a major stoplight in Raleigh and there were people all around the van. Half the wedding party had come outside and cars were stopping all over the road. I could hear sirens from a police car barreling down the road toward us. I jumped out and said, "Everybody, back up! I think we have a live dead body in here!"

They just looked at me more confused than a wiener dog in a bun factory. Amy jumped out and pulled the stretcher from the van. All you could see was a body with blood all over it. But it was still moving and groaning and had both hands covering its face. The policeman ran up and wanted to know what was going on; people were all around us trying to see; and there I was with Amy, standing over a stretcher of what I thought was supposed to be a dead man turned zombie. Then he moved his hands and I saw the dead man was Jason.

Seems he had called Amy when he heard my little plan, and they had made a plan of their own. Problem was, when Jason closed the bag, he zipped it too far and couldn't let himself back out. Well, I learned a long time ago that the early bird gets the worm—but the late bird never gets shot. And if you're gonna get one over on the Ronster, you'd better be slicker than a skinned Georgia catfish soaked in baby oil.

I had beat Jason so bad with that broom he looked like he had run a forty-yard dash in a thirty-yard barn full of razor blades. He was split wide open and needed some stitches in his face—not to mention I had broken some of his fingers.

Amy was trying to explain the whole thing to the cop just as the news van pulled up and the reporters jumped out. The cop caught on and started trying to disperse the crowd while the reporter was trying to talk to me and find out what had just happened. Amy helped Jason back into the van and said, "Come on. I've got to call work and tell them I have to take him to the hospital."

I said, "Baby, after that I'd rather fight a pack of wild tigers in the dark with a switch than to ever get back in that van. I'll call a cab and meet y'all at the hospital."

Jason was still pretty much out of it. Amy strapped him in the stretcher and pushed it back into the van, then sped off with the police car giving her an escort. I just stood there with the news guy, who kept asking me to explain what had happened.

"Bo," I told him, "I'm not real sure. But I can tell you I'd rather jump off a ten-foot ladder into a five-gallon bucket of calf slobber than to ever go through something like that again. I did learn one thing, though."

"Please tell the viewing audience what you learned, sir."

"I learned there ain't no sense in beating a dead horse—but apparently it can't hurt none neither."

Then I tried to flag down a cab.

[Uglier]

1. He looks like his face was on fire and someone put it out with the spiked side of a golf shoe.

2. He looks like he was inside the outhouse when lightning struck.

3. He looks like someone beat him in the head with an iron pot full of melted quarters.

4. Her face looks like she played goalie for a darts team.

5. She's got summer teeth: summer over here and summer over there.

6. Her teeth are so crooked, she could eat corn on the cob through a picket fence.

7. He couldn't get laid in a monkey whorehouse with a fistful of bananas.

8. Her butt looks like squirrels fighting over a walnut in a burlap sack.

9. If she went skinny-dippin', you could skim ugly off the water for about a week.

10. She might as well wipe her tail with a wagon wheel; there ain't no end to that, either.

11. He couldn't get laid if he crawled up a hen's tail and waited.

12. She looks like she's been drug backward through a knothole.

13. It looks like two Buicks fighting for a parking place in the back of dem jeans.

14. Bo, that's a moped girl: the kind you wanna ride but you don't want your friends to catch you on.

15. That's way too much pumpkin for a nickel.

16. She looks rougher than a two-dollar hooker on dollar day.

17. That girl could run a fat rat off a cheesecake.

18. That girl is so ugly, her stare could chip paint.

19. Uglier than the east end of a horse heading west.

20. Uglier than a burnt stump.

21. Ugly as homemade sin.

22. She was definitely born downwind from the outhouse.

23. He's uglier than a melted turd over a hot stack of pancakes.

24. She's so ugly, she could make a Chihuahua break a bull chain.

25. He's so ugly, when he was a kid his momma borrowed a baby to bring to church.

26. She's uglier than a hat full of buttholes at a bean-eating contest.

27. She's uglier than a stuck duck in a dry pond.

28. He's uglier than a spit can full of smashed buttholes.

29. He's uglier than a five-gallon bucket of hairy armpits.

30. She looks like something the dog drug out from under the porch.

25

If I Tell You a Rooster Can Pull a Freight Train . . . You'd Better Hook 'Im Up

When I finally got Lizard Lick Towing off the ground and we started making waves in the repossession industry, I figured I'd bring my best friend, Johnny Perry, on with me. See, Johnny was a little intimidating: he was a mountain of a man with twenty-six-inch biceps, and he looked meaner than a Keebler elf who was demoted to food-packing. Now, Johnny was country as cornflakes and gooder than grits. but because of his size and strength he could tear up a railroad truck with a rubber mallet. So I began training him in the tricks and trade of the repossession industry.

One night after dark I set out in my new truck, fitted with an auto-loader lift specially made to perform repossessions. I was driving, one of my agents was in the middle, and Johnny manned the passenger door. We were packed in there tighter than three wet rats in a wool sock. The night started out slowly with us cruising around, looking for a Chevy 1500 truck. We eased down the street where the debtor lived and creeped by the address. I spotted the truck nosed-in against a wood fence with a car on the right of it and a Ford Ranger pulled crossways behind it. This debtor knew we were coming and had his truck blocked in tighter than a bull's butt in the middle of fly season.

My agent sized up the situation and said, "Well, you can't get 'em all." He was ready to give up. But ol' Johnny said, "Oh yes, you can!"

The agent looked at Johnny. "You think you can get that truck?" Johnny replied, "Does Howdy Doody got wooden balls?"

It was at that point I knew I'd rather stare at the sun with binoculars than ask Johnny what he was thinking. But before I could say a word, he slid out of my truck faster than green grass through a greased goose.

Johnny started walking down the driveway toward the vehicles as me and the agent sat staring at him in wonder. Now, remember: ol' Johnny was stronger than mule piss with the foam farted off. He just walked over to the back of that Ranger, reached down, and picked its whole back end up in the air. Then he started walking backward, pulling the truck across the yard, making more noise than two skeletons scroggin' on a tin roof using a beer can for protection. All of a sudden the porch light flicked on, the door swung open, and there stood a man who looked hotter than two grizzlies fighting in a forest fire. And he had a six-shooter in his right hand!

My tail drew up tighter than a gnat's butt stretched over an oil drum. That debtor burst through the door at a full run, gun raised, screaming like someone just stole his Oreos. Then he saw Johnny standing there, halfway across the yard, with the truck in the air, arms bulging, staring right back at him.

Johnny said, "Mister, I hope that revolver got eight shots, 'cause six ain't gonna do nothin' but piss me off!"

It seemed like time froze. The guy was standing there looking at Johnny holding that truck in the air, and his eyes looked like a raccoon's in the spotlight after getting caught in the corn bin.

Johnny continued, "Well, you gonna shoot? Or you just gonna stand there lookin' stupid?"

Without saying a word, the debtor turned and walked back into the house. I sat perfectly still. Johnny started to pull the Ranger the rest of the way out of the driveway so I could back up to the Chevy. Just then, the screen door slung open. I immediately thought, *This guy went and got a bigger gun*—until I saw him just toss a set of keys toward Johnny. Then he shut the door and switched off the outside light.

Johnny walked over to the 1500, cranked it up, and pulled it out of the yard. When he drove up beside me he was grinning like a possum eating crap out of a light socket. He rolled the window down, looked at the agent and me, and said, "If I tell you a rooster can pull a freight train, you'd better hook 'em up!" And with that, he put the Chevy in drive and headed back to the shop with his first repossession.

[More Advice]

1. Never kick a fresh turd on a hot day.

2. If you're riding ahead of the herd, look behind you and make sure it's still there.

3. Never wrestle with a pig. Chances are you'll get dirty and the pig will like it.

4. Ride hard, shoot straight, and always speak the truth.

5. If you're gonna take cattle to town, do it on Sunday. There's less traffic and fewer people to fight.

6. Never sell your mule in order to buy a plow.

7. Psycho women are like herpes. You never get rid of them and they're a real pain.

8. Never try to teach a pig to dance. You just waste your time . . . and you're gonna annoy the pig.

9. Don't let your mouth talk you right outta life.

10. Sometimes it's better to keep your mouth shut and let people think you're an idiot than open it and prove 'em right.

11. When you were born, you were crying and everyone around you was smiling. Live your life so that when you die, you're smiling and everyone around you is crying.

12. Before you borrow money from a friend, decide which you need more.

13. If you think you're somebody, try bossing your neighbor's dog around.

14. If you take a drug test and it comes back negative, you'd better get on the phone with your dealer.

15. If you wanna go nowhere in life, try following the crowd.

16. Live your life in such a way that men hate ya, women love ya, and little kids all over the world wanna be just like ya.

26

Some Days You're the Pigeon . . . And Some Days You're the Statue

For years I had been trying to get my pops to change his hunting habits and venture into using a muzzle loader or a bow rather than a conventional rifle. The seasons where the bow or muzzle loader could be used came much earlier in the year, and the hunting was much more difficult—and, therefore, much more rewarding. Needless to say, changing Pops is about as easy as nailing a raw egg to a tree with a sledgehammer. About two months before muzzle-loading season, my years of pestering him finally paid off and he gave in. I was more excited than a three-armed nanny at a cross-stitch convention, so I went out and got him a top-notch muzzle loader with a scope that could see the smile on Lincoln's face in the back pocket of a tight pair of jeans.

I never anticipated so much griping and bellyaching! As we set that jewel in at a hundred yards, he complained about everything from the mule kick when firing to the color of the targets we were shooting at. I might as well have been wiping my tail with a wagon wheel, 'cause there ain't no end to that, either. But I made it through and got the inline tradition dialed in so tight you could've shot the balls off a dragonfly in a nosedive.

Now, the spot I hunted was a real honey hole. You could poke your eye out with a blunt stick and still see plenty of big ol' bucks. I've shot several out of that patch of woods that were two ax handles wide across the horns. So when opening day arrived, I was more tickled than a speckled trout at a pole-dot painting party. I had Pops a great spot overlooking a bottleneck where the deer love to funnel through near the edge of a pond before heading out to a cornfield.

Now, I ain't saying I'm one of the best hunters in the world, but out of the ten best, six of 'em are on my fan page. It was busier than a horsefly in a Hoover that morning, and the deer were everywhere. I sat a ground blind about a hundred yards from Pops and was trying to see what was moving where. I wanted to point out that you can't hang a key ring and hat at the same time.

Well, about nine a.m., I saw a bruiser coming out of the cut about sixty yards away from me, heading straight at Pops. I was as nervous as a fat bee at a flyswatter convention. I just knew that any second I was gonna hear the pop of the cap and the blast of that black-powder muzzle loader, and Pops would start making more noise than a Sherman tank in a peanut-brittle factory. But after an hour of silence, I saw Pops coming up through the woods.

"Pops, didn't you see that vanilla gorilla with cream horns pass by?"

"Nah—I seen nothin' but squirrels and foxes."

Now, it was about that time I started to think he couldn't see a set of bull's balls if he was standing between its hind legs.

"I must've seen twenty-five doe or more," I told him. "You're blinder than a rugby bat at midnight!"

Wasn't much more to do that morning, so we went and got lunch, then headed back early that afternoon to get settled in before the deer started moving. By about an hour before dark I had, once again, seen enough deer to run a maggot off a four-day-old gut barrel. None of them were real shooters, though, so I broke out a grunt call, which simulates a buck who's marking his territory. These grunts let all the other deer around know he's the big dog in the local pound. Well, no sooner had I hit that jewel for a few blasts when out to my right steps a massive eight-pointer with the most beautiful set of chocolate horns. He was all bristled up and madder than a one-armed paperhanger with jock itch.

He marched forty yards below me, in line with the creek I was overlooking, which fed right into the corner of the pond Pops was at. So once again I let a shooter walk, knowing Pops was getting ready to lay the smack down with that ol' smoke pole. And once again, about an hour went by with nothing but silence. Finally, I saw Pops tromping through the woods with his flashlight on.

"How did you not see that deer?" I asked him. And as I told him what I saw and where that deer went, I saw him squint his eyes.

He said, "So you mean to tell me you not only grunted a deer in during muzzle-loader season, but you passed up a shooter buck in the same day?"

It was at this point I realized he thought I was lying like a cheap rug in a Laundromat.

He continued, "I didn't see no deer . . . especially no bucks. Are you sure you're not stretching the truth a little?"

"Pops, when it comes to hunting, I'm as honest as the day is long—and I got over twenty head mounts to back my play."

"Well, OK, then. Tomorrow morning I'm sitting with you." I agreed with about as much excitement as a dead pig in the sunshine.

So the next morning we headed in—both of us—to sit in my one-man ground blind. Now, the first thing I noticed was that Pops made more noise than a blind fox in a hen-house. When we got to the blind, it was a sight to see two fully grown men trying to squeeze into a small ground tent with two chairs, two guns, two backpacks, and a cooler. After getting madder than a wet hen with hemorrhoids, I said, "Let me set all my stuff outside and just sit on the ground beside you, so we have room."

Finally, we got settled in and I was as comfortable as a fat turkey at the slaughterhouse the day before Thanksgiving. Then I started realizing why he hadn't been seeing any deer: he never stopped moving around! I couldn't figure out if he had a bee in his bonnet or ants in his pants, but he was louder than a drunken cowboy in a whorehouse on dollar day.

Sure enough, we hadn't seen anything all morning because of Pops, and he was glaring at me like a hoot owl over a barrel of mice. Then I remembered my grunt call and whispered to him that I was going to give it a few blows and he should be looking around. I pointed to where that big eight-point came from the evening before.

Well, you'd have thought I was about to shoot the governor and hang his wife. Pops started in on me like a bear eating bumblebees. So I did what any self-respecting hunter would've done: I started blowing that grunt call. See, it wasn't that I didn't hear Pops; I just didn't care what he had to say. And at this point, anything was better than his yapping. I'd got no more than the first few grunts out when that ol' eight-pointer broke out in a full run from almost the exact spot as the night before.

Pops looked like the cat that ate the canary. We started scrambling around like two blind mice in a round room looking for a corner while trying to set up on this buck. I had Pops ease his smoke pole out the front window and gave him a stick with a fork on the end to prop it on. That deer started walking the same path as the evening before, so I whispered to Pops, "When he gets to the big stump, squeeze off on him. I'll try to grunt to stop him. But let me know before you shoot, 'cause my head is right beside your barrel."

If you've ever heard a black-powder gun go off, you'll know it's louder than two trains having a head-on in a bell factory, and it shoots a huge flame from the end of the barrel and a big balloon of smoke that you have to wait to clear before you can see if you hit anything. To top it off, you get one shot and then you have to pull the rod from under the barrel, pour the powder down the barrel, stick a patch under the bullet, ram it down the barrel, pack it with the rod, and put a cap on the firing mechanism to shoot it again. Needless to say, it's easier to herd blind chickens in the dark.

So Pops had his gun out the window with the hammer pulled back. I was right beside him, getting ready to blow the grunt. Just before the buck got to the stump—*Boom!* The percussion of the blast blew out my left eardrum. I was dizzier than a drunk man in a house of mirrors. I couldn't breathe 'cause of all the smoke, and there was Pops shaking me and screaming, "Reload my gun! Reload my gun!"

Now it was pretty close to dark and he had forgotten the flashlight. And I was more confused than a milk cow on Astroturf as I fumbled through his bag for the powder and caps and bullets. He was all over me like a blind hog on corn, screaming at me—though I couldn't hear but out of one ear. I tried to pack his gun and look for the deer, and just then I saw its head pop up and then go down again. I said, "Pops, he's still moving."

So he yanked the gun from my hand—I'm not even sure the bullets were all the way down. Then Pops starts screaming, "Where's he at? Where's he at?"

Now, I know Pops was more excited than a four-armed monkey with two peters, but at that point I personally would've rather been superglued to a chimpanzee with a blowtorch in a powder house. I said, "Pops, let me get out; I'll stand up and shoot him for you." I grabbed my binoculars and went to get out of the ground blind.

Pops said, "Son, you got a better chance of putting socks on a rooster than getting out and scaring my deer off."

"You're right, Pops. The ear-splitting boom of the gun, along with your whooping and hollering and romping around in here like a pair of wild dogs in a pizza parlor didn't scare him a bit, but me stepping outside is sure to run him off."

So I leaned out the window with my binoculars and spotted that deer down in the creek. I had my head all the way out the window and was side by side with the end of the gun, trying to tell Pops where to look.

"See the stump, Pops?"

"Yeah."

"See the small tree three yards to the right?"

"Yeah."

"Come down about five yards this side of the creek. But tell me before you're gonna—"

Boom! He set off another round.

This time, not only was I gagging from the smoke like a fat baby on sour milk, but he had powder-burned the whole left side of my face! I started rolling around in the dirt quicker than a fat rat on a cheesecake, trying to put the burning out on my face. The way I was carrying on you'd have thought someone shot our Sunday mule. I jumped up looking like an ol' beat dog someone had kept under a porch. I was about to tell Pops if brains were cotton he couldn't Kotex a flea, but his eyes were bigger than a puppy dog with his first Milk-Bone—and they were full of tears.

He grabbed me in a huge bear hug and said, "I got 'im son—no, we got 'im. You helped me get my first big buck!"

Well, even though the whole ordeal was as much fun as a nosebleed, I smile like a possum eating persimmons every time I walk into his house and see that mount.

You know, some days you're the pigeon and some days you're the statue. I guess that day, I was both.

[Confused]

1. He's as confused as an Amish electrician.
2. He was so confused he didn't know whether to scratch his watch or wind his butt.
3. He looked as confused as a monkey trying to do a math problem.
4. He's as confused as a cow on Astroturf.
5. He's as confused as a cross-eyed 'coon trying to cross the road.
6. He's more confused than a turtle on the center stripe.
7. He's as confused as a blind man at a silent movie.
8. He's as confused as a tailless cow during fly season.
9. He's as confused as a noseless rat at a cheese mill.
10. He's as baffled as Adam on Mother's Day.

[Tight]

1. Tighter than a bull's tail on fight night.
2. Tighter than a frog's butt—and that's watertight.
3. Tighter than a minister's wife's girdle at an all-you-can-eat pancake breakfast.
4. Tighter than a mosquito's butt in a nosedive.
5. Tighter than socks on a rooster.
6. Tighter than a camel's butt in a sand storm.
7. Tighter than Siamese ticks on a dead hound dog.

[Nervous]

1. Nervous as a long-tailed cat in a room full of rocking chairs.
2. Nervous as a pit bull crapping thumbtacks on a balloon ride.
3. Nervous as a dog crappin' peach pits in a penthouse.
4. Nervous as a sugar-dipped pony on an anthill.
5. Nervous as a fat bee at a flyswatter convention.

[Busy]

1. Busier than a five-legged cat trying to cover crap on a marble floor.
2. Busier than a stump full of fire ants in a flash flood.
3. Busier than a one-armed paperhanger with crabs.
4. Busier than a funeral-home fan in July.
5. Busier than a borrowed mule.
6. Busier than a dog with two peckers.
7. Busier than a bumblebee in a bucket of tar.
8. Busier than a horsefly in a Hoover.
9. Busier than a blind dog at a cat pound.
10. Busier than a banana salesman at a monkey whorehouse.
11. He's so busy, you'd think he was twins.

27

A Fisherman Is a Jerk on One End of the Line Waiting for a Jerk on the Other

After my cousin Brian was married and finally settled down, he bought himself a nice little house in a subdivision outside Lizard Lick. When Brian bought the house he didn't know that he was the only backwoods plowboy living in the neighborhood. He'd looked at the house on a weekday and then woke up on a Saturday and realized he was alone. Most of the folks there were Wall Street types, suit-and-tie guys. But it really didn't matter to Brian or me.

Well, it was pretty obvious that Brian stood out like a set of twenty-four-inch gold rims at a Puff Daddy concert. Of course, I made Larry the Cable Guy look like a debutante. I had this big, jacked-up truck with a deer painted on the hood and COUNTRY BOY CAN SURVIVE on the tailgate. I have always believed in respecting your heritage. I used to run around concerts screaming "Captain Redneck!"

One Saturday, I asked Brian to take me fishing. He'd bought a brand-new boat, and I told him I'd found the perfect fishing hole at the Little River Reservoir, which was at the head of the Eno River near Durham, North Carolina. Brian was really proud of his fishing boat. He paid $30,000 for the boat and there wasn't a scratch on it. Now, to us this was akin to an eighty-foot Riviera yacht, and that boat cost just about as much as his house. See, down here you don't judge a man by the car he's driving or the house he lives in; you wanna know how a country boy is doing you just look at his boat and his barn. I showed up at Brian's house and blew my truck's horn. It played "Dixie," and Brian's neighbors probably thought it was the Dukes of Hazzard about to have a hoedown with a toe down pulling up.

The Little River Reservoir has three natural hot springs that boiled up in it, so the fish grew year-round since it was warm water. I knew there were some huge fish in that hole—some so big they would make you cut your vision on your eyetooth just trying to look at them. I was more excited than a large-mouth bass at an earthworm reunion about fishing there. But the reason it was such a great place to fish is because nobody could get to it. There wasn't a boat ramp, and you had to go through a swamp to get there. I thought Brian was going to kill me as we made our way to the reservoir. There were tree limbs and stumps tearing up the side of his boat the whole way. We looked like two swamp-fed billy goats by the time we got to the drop spot, and the boat looked like it had a custom paint job—only it was camo! Brian was hotter than a gasoline cat walking through hell with a kerosene tail.

We finally got out there, and I wanted to fish at the head of the Eno River because that's where the stripers were running. But the head of the river was located right next to this big hydroelectric dam. When the stripers are running, they run all the way to the dam and then they're penned up. They have nowhere to go except on a hook! Now, that ain't really fishing, but we eat what we catch and I figured I could fill in a month's worth of freezer meat right there.

A couple of days earlier, the engineers had opened the floodgates, so the water was really deep. When we pulled up to the dam, I knew Brian was worried. There were big signs everywhere that said Danger. Stay Away. But I figured that was for the guys with the little johnboats. We had us a genuine, bona fide bass boat with more horsepower than a Kentucky Derby turn four. Brian had his boat wide open as we were sitting right in front of the dam. We were practically sitting still because his boat didn't have a chance against the strong currents. So here we are, full-throttle, and the boat is sitting still. Now, to an old redneck this was more fun than tying cats by the tail over a clothesline and spraying 'em with a water hose. The action was on and I knew the fish were about to be bountiful!

"Bo, there are some big fish right here!" I told Brian.

"Do you not see those signs?" Brian asked me. "We aren't even supposed to be here!"

I was fishing the whole time. I was throwing out rattle-traps, and he was trying to stay up with the currents. I was having more fun than a Labrador retriever at a duck-calling contest. After a few minutes, Brian had seen enough and laid the law down.

"You can fish, but you're gonna do it from a life preserver," Brian said. "So this is the time you decide whether you wanna sink or swim."

Now, I'm not partial to thirty-mile-an-hour water, especially if I'm the falling tree. So I reluctantly agreed to head back to the smoother side of the lake and we started trying to maneuver our way back to land. But then I saw a doe swimming across the water. Now, just about that time you could have backstroked it all the way to the front door. I figured I'd be the first guy on the block to catch a pet deer.

"Bo, pull up beside him!" I told Brian.

He looked at me and told me I was as crazy as a methadone house mouse. But Brian was smaller than me, so I rolled up on him like a fifty-foot section of sod and kindly convinced him that he'd rather be in hell with a broken back and jock itch than to not cooperate.

Brian pulled the boat up closer to the deer. He thought I only wanted to look at it.

"Bo, I want to catch him!" I told Brian. "I'm going to lasso him and put him in the boat."

Of course, I didn't know how crazy a live deer gets. I collared a rope around the deer's neck and it was madder than graffiti with a sore throat! I pulled the deer up into the boat, and I would have rather been an armless man watching porn than to go toe to toe with a live doe, though I didn't quite know that just yet.

The deer started chasing us around the boat, and we were running around like our hair was on fire and our tails were catching. Who knew a deer could be meaner than three-horned billy goats during mating season? The deer started kicking and was knocking holes all over Brian's new boat. The deer was snapping fishing poles, tearing up the upholstery on the seats, and shattering glass windshields. The deer just went ballistic. You would rather have been duct-taped to a moose's belly during rutting season. But I was happier than a leech at a blood bank because I had a pet deer. I just had to figure out how to lasso it again, but Brian wouldn't stop scaring it. The deer was kicking like a bronco, and Brian was screaming like a thirteen-year-old girl at a Justin Bieber concert.

Brian finally jumped on the bow of the boat and persuaded me to put the deer back in the water. Now, that presented a slight problem. It's a whole lot easier letting the cat out of the bag than putting it back in. There are two things you can't do in this world: survive an atomic blast and put toothpaste back in a tube. What's a third thing you can't do? You can't corral a deer in a boat.

Brian and I were sitting in a boat with a deer and were

as confused as Confucius on crack. It was just like in the movies. Every time I took a step toward the deer, it started screaming again. How in the world were we going to get the deer out of the boat? Finally, I took a fishing rod and smacked the deer in the rear with it. The deer took off running right toward Brian, who was standing on the bow. The deer hit Brian so hard that when he finally woke up, his clothes were back in style. The deer flew to the left, and Brian flew to the right—right off the boat and into the water.

Since we were sitting in only four feet of water, I thought there was just one thing to do—try to corral the deer again. But Brian was screaming at me to bring the boat to him, so needless to say, the deer got away.

Since we hadn't caught a fish all afternoon, I persuaded Brian to drive forty-five minutes away to put the boat in the ocean. By now the boat had substantial deer damage and Brian was tore up from the floor up. I told him that with some duct tape, superglue, Bondo, and paint, we could fix anything. But all he wanted was a twelve-pack and some aspirin, so we went by a store and grabbed that and a bottle of 'shine. We stopped and picked up my brother, Jason, and headed for the sound to finally do some serious fishing.

Now, keep in mind that Brian's boat didn't have GPS—or any windshields after the deer attack—so we had to rely on compasses. And we'd never been fishing in the ocean, other than on charter trips.

"Y'all just cruise around the inlet, and I'm going to go below and ease the pain and take a break," Brian said.

Now, I don't think Brian was upset because his boat looked like a sixty-year-old hooker at a frat house. He had to go home and explain to his wife, Tracy, what happened, so he was going to ingest all the liquid courage he could find. Brian headed below and I took one look at Jason. With a grin on our faces bigger than pit-cooked pig, we pointed that baby due east to the Gulf Stream.

See, I'd already been drinking all day, and I knew the redfish were about thirty miles offshore. The compass said we were headed east, so I figured all we had to do to get back was head west. It was really simple—even to a guy who had as much navigational sense as a dead mule.

Brian was below with the music blaring, washing his troubles away. I always told him, don't try to drown your troubles in liquor 'cause troubles know how to swim. I put that boat in full speed. We were hitting three- and four-foot whitecaps. It was tearing his boat to pieces. When Brian finally came up and stepped out of the cabin, he could only see water. There wasn't any land in sight. He went ballistic. We didn't have any safety equipment. The deer tore up the radio and there was water coming in the sides of the boat from the holes the deer left.

We were arguing with Brian about going back to shore. But then I saw a huge cloud come up next to the boat.

"Did y'all see that?" I said. "Did y'all see that? What in the world was that?"

The only fishing poles we had on the boat were bait casters for bass; we didn't have any real ocean rods. I saw this big swirl come next to the boat again. Brian's boat was twenty-three feet long and this animal was as big as the boat. It was the biggest animal I'd ever seen. Bo, I intended to land that critter like the old man in the sea and tie it off to the boat and make history.

"Go! Go!" I yelled to Brian. "Get me next to that fish!"

I had Gotcha plugs and I threw one out to set a hook in the critter. I snagged him! I threw another plug out and then another one. By the time I was finished, I'd snagged that critter with four poles. All the poles were bent over, bobbing up and down, and about to break in half. I ran into the cabin and found Brian's daddy's ocean rod. It had a huge treble hook on it. It looked like a collard green on Miracle-Gro.

I threw out the treble hook and snagged the critter again. This time, the critter got hotter than an ol' sitting hen setting eggs in a wool basket in the summertime. It turned around and rammed the front of the boat. The front of the boat literally stood up out of the water. I still don't know how that boat didn't flip.

I finally saw what I'd snagged: a twenty-foot basking shark. They're not meat-eaters, so I wasn't worried. There wasn't any way I was going to bring in a basking shark, but I didn't know any better because I'd been drinking all day. I even grabbed the anchor and tried to snag the shark again to tie it to the boat. I figured the anchor would be a big enough hook to wear him down. Of course, I was never known for my massive intellect. But as I was fighting the shark, Brian was flipping like a dolphin at Sea World during a fish-feeding show. Then Brian did the unthinkable as I was wrestling this mammoth like Hulk Hogan on Ric Flair: he ran up to the front of the boat and cut all my lines.

"Bo, what are you doing?" I screamed.

"Saving my boat," Brian said.

After that, I was hotter than a tick on a dog's testicles. We argued for about an hour, and then it took us about four more hours to get back to shore. When we finally got Brian's battered boat loaded back onto a trailer, a couple of game wardens drove up to us.

"Did y'all catch anything?" they asked.

"No, but we had the biggest fish in the world hooked," I told them. "It was a basking shark."

They started laughing at us.

"You know what would have happened if you'd pulled up here with a basking shark?" one of the game wardens asked me. "You would have faced about ten years in prison and a fifty-thousand-dollar fine. A basking shark is an endangered species."

Well, Brian looked at me and I looked at Jason and we all just looked at the boat or what was left of it. After about a minute, I looked back at the game wardens.

I said, "Y'all know what we all learned here today? That a fisherman is a jerk on one end of the line waiting for a jerk on the other."

And with that we headed back to suburbia to deal with Brian's wife.

[Redneck Ponderings]

1. Do infants enjoy infancy as much as adults enjoy adultery?

2. What do you call a male ladybug?

3. If you choke a Smurf, what color does it turn?

4. Can vegetarians eat animal crackers?

5. If the No. 2 pencil is the most popular, then why is it still No. 2?

6. If a turtle doesn't have a shell, is he homeless or naked?

7. What if the Hokey Pokey is *really* what it's all about?

8. Would a fly without wings be called a walk?

9. How come "abbreviated" is such a long word?

10. If quitters never win and winners never quit, what fool came up with "Quit while you're ahead"?

11. How much deeper would oceans be if sponges didn't live there?

12. Despite the cost of living, have you noticed how popular it remains?

13. If you try to fail and succeed, which have you done?

14. If Barbie is so popular, why do you have to buy her friends?

15. If someone with multiple personalities threatens to kill himself, is it a hostage situation?

16. Isn't it a bit unnerving that doctors call what they do a "practice"?

17. What do you do when you see an endangered animal eating an endangered plant?

28

Sometimes You Can't Tell Nobody Nuthin' . . . That Ain't Never Been Nowhere

One of the toughest repos I've ever attempted was actually on some vehicles belonging to a funeral home. I received an order to repossess both the hearse and the family car. Now, it just seemed to me that bad karma was on the horizon if we got those vehicles, but my job is to find and take anything that floats, flies, sinks, rolls, or swims. Besides—no matter how you clean a skunk, he's still gonna stink, so I figured, since at the time I was as broke as the Ten Commandments, I'd better figure out how to get the hearse and car.

I also felt that, with as much as those places charge for a permanent bed and a plot of ground, the only place they were gonna find any sympathy around here was between "symbolic" and "syphilis" in the family dictionary. So I started trying to figure out how I was gonna get both vehicles and do it in a respectful manner.

Several times a day I'd ease past this funeral home, but I never could locate the vehicles outside. So one night, I decided to park down the street and sneak around some, to get a better layout of the place and see if I could spot them. Sure enough, when I eased around back of the garage and peeked in, I could see them both sitting inside, shining and prettier than a freshly cooked baked-bean sandwich. So day after day and night after night, I continued to try to catch those vehicles outside. I knew there was always more than one way to choke a dog than by just feeding it peanut butter, so I started devising a way to get to the vehicles—since they weren't coming out to me.

Now, it just so happens that my wife, Amy, is a licensed mortician. But I would rather eat a cold scab sandwich and wash it down with a mug of snot than to give her the satisfaction of figuring this one out before I did. She told me, "Ronnie, they are only gonna pull them out for cleaning and for use, so your methods are gonna be about as useful as a dog with no legs."

But I'm the type of guy who will hang in there like a hair in a biscuit until I get the job done. So I figured I'd wait till there was a wake, sneak in with the crowd, ease out to the garage, locate the keys, hit the door opener, and then make like a tree in the fall and leave. If I took one of my guys with me, we could even drive both vehicles out at the same time. We could pull all this off and no one would even know, 'cause they'd all be inside.

I proudly announced to Amy that I had a foolproof plan, and I went into detail about my covert operation. Amy busted out laughing and told me it would never work. She started to tell me why, but by then I was hotter than if I'd been playing hot potato in the Sahara Desert because she'd shot my idea down. So I told her, "Honey, I'm riding this chicken. You're just holding the head."

She said, "OK. But don't say I didn't warn you." And she left, laughing hysterically.

So I called my tow manager and cousin, Brian, and told him my plan. Then I started watching the obituaries, bound and determined to prove to Amy that, when it comes to repossessions, she couldn't hold water if she was carrying a ten-gallon bucket.

After a few days, there it was: a seven p.m. wake at the funeral home. I called Brian and told him to dally up; we had an old friend we had to pay our last respects to. Now, you have to keep in mind: Brian is straight off the farm. The only thing he wears bigger than his belt buckle is his hat. And my neck is redder than nine miles of Georgia asphalt on a summer Sunday, so we tend to stand out just a tad. Brian showed up at the house decked out in his best John Wayne lookalike duds and Amy said, "Are y'all really gonna attempt this?"

I said, "Does a fat puppy hate fast cars? In an hour you'll be gagging on crow—and I ain't giving you no gravy to dull the flavor!"

She just smiled and said, "When you come back empty-handed, let me know, and I'll get 'em for you."

Now, at that point it was personal: she was calling me out, and I would have rather slid down a barbed-wire banister with a bucket of alcohol than to come back without at least one car. So off we went. I got a real uneasy feeling when we pulled into the parking lot around seven thirty p.m. The place was packed. There must have been more than a hundred vehicles in the parking lot, so at least it would be really busy and no one would notice us snooping around. We got out of Brian's jacked-up, extended-cab Chevy truck (which happened to be the biggest truck in the lot, but we just figured everyone drove their Sunday vehicles). This guy in a suit opened the door for us and we rolled on inside. The entire lobby was empty. The doorman said, "Everyone is already inside the room. Go to the third door on the left." At this point, we were as confused as a turtle on the center stripe, but since there was no way for us to sneak around, we headed to the room. Well, we opened the door and walked in, and it was right then I knew why Amy found so much humor in us going to this wake. I didn't realize that the funeral home specialized in certain religions, and it seemed me and Brian had just walked right into a Buddhist funeral!

There were all these people in orange robes singing these weird chants with all this incense burning. When we walked in, I was wound tigher than a three-day clock. There me and Brian were with the facial expressions of two mules eating briars. And you could have called the dogs and pissed on the campfire when one of the priests walked up and asked how we knew the deceased. Before I could simply say we were just in the wrong room, Brian spouted out, "Oh he was my momma's cousin." I don't know what bothered me more: the fact it was obvious we weren't related or the fact I forgot to tell Brian the wake was for a lady. Needless to say, I left him standing there like he was so ugly his momma had to feed him from a slingshot.

When Brian finally got back to the truck, he was grinning at me like a baked possum for Sunday lunch. Sometimes I actually wonder if Brian could put a gopher back in a wet hole. But regardless, I knew I had to go back and face Amy, and I would've rather been set on fire and put out with the bottom of a golf shoe than to watch her gloat.

When I arrived home she was sitting on the couch smiling ear to ear. Right next to her was a life-sized mannequin. Now, at this point, I was feeling like I wanted to take a long walk in front of a short bus, and I wasn't about to ask her any questions. She stood up and said, "I don't see a hearse outside." Me and Brian just looked down sheepishly as she continued: "Just sit down, boys, and I'll show you how to lick this repo."

First, she told me and Brian to go lay the mannequin in the bed and cover him with a sheet. Then she grabbed the phone and called the funeral home. She explained to them that she had a pickup and needed the hearse because the family was on the premises. When I heard this plan, I was as happy as a bucked-tooth horse eating corn cobs through a picket fence. Amy told us they always leave the keys in the car on pickup, and so she sent Brian outside to hide around the side of the house while I stayed inside to make sure nothing got out of hand.

Sure enough, two guys in suits pulled up and Amy led them through the house. They had the stretcher for the mannequin. When we got to the bedroom and pulled the sheet back, both of their jaws dropped so far you could've filled the space with ten dollars' worth of forty-cent jaw-breakers. Both those fellows were as confused as noseless rats at the cheese mill. Amy explained to them we had a repossession on the hearse, and by the expressions on their faces, I knew for sure that they were gonna be madder than a bobcat tied up in a piss fire. In the meantime, Brian had already gotten into the car and was headed down the road. He called in on the cell phone to let us know he was clear. I was gearing up for a Texas tussle with these two rather large fellows when, in the most eloquent voice, the larger one said, "I knew something was amiss when we walked in, because we have never done a Caucasian family. I should have caught on. You, ma'am, are a very innovative agent."

I chimed in, proud as a heifer of her first calf, and said, "Yep, that ol' girl is slicker than a hound dog's fake tooth." Everybody just looked at me like I had kicked a cat.

Amy went on to tell them we also now had their stretchers, and she knew they had a graveside the next day, so the only way they could have them back was to give us the family car also. The bigger guy spoke again: "You must be aware that, due to ethics, I can't cause a scene or I'll be in jeopardy of a reprimand by the state board."

Amy smiled and politely responded, "Yes, I'm a licensed mortician and funeral director. That's why I knew how to handle this situation. In this business, it's not always power and lead that gets the job done."

Amy said she was leaving with those two guys to get the family car back at the funeral home. Now, the expression on my face must've been a sight, 'cause to me she added, "Ronnie, if I had a dog that looked like you did right now, I'd shave his butt and make him walk backwards."

The rest of the week I couldn't even look at Amy. Her mouth was running more than a boardinghouse toilet. She told everybody about her repo and how she had pulled one off that even the great Ron and Brian couldn't get.

I must admit I had to swallow a lot of crow that week. After two days I finally broke down and asked her why she let me make such a fool of myself. Why didn't she just tell me about the inner workings of funeral homes instead of letting me look like the dog who caught the parked car?

Amy just smiled and said, "Baby, I tried. But sometimes you can't tell nobody nuthin' that ain't never been nowhere."

[Even More Ronosophy]

1. Every path has some puddles; some are just deeper than others.

2. Lazy and Quarrelsome are ugly sisters.

3. Scars are just tattoos with better stories.

4. Even a dog knows the difference between being kicked and being stepped on.

5. Trailer-park trash: too much breeding, not enough reading.

6. Give a man a free hand and he's sure to run it all over ya.

7. If you wanna know how country people are doing, don't look at the house, look at the barn.

8. There's more ways to choke a dog than just feeding him peanut butter.

9. I'll remember the things I've done for a while, but I'll remember the people I did them with forever.

10. You can turn a housewife into a whore but you'll never turn a whore into a housewife.

11. There's more than one way to skin a catfish on a Friday night.

12. A cat will always blink when you hit it over the head with a sledgehammer.

13. One hundred percent of all divorces start with marriage.

29

I Used to Have a Handle on Life . . . But Now It's Broken

Through all the years I've spent in the repossession business, I have learned the most valuable asset you can have is your wits. Problem is, in most situations you encounter you really can't have a battle of wits, 'cause the other person is usually only half armed. So the next best thing is to have someone watching your back out there in the field. And in all my years, I have to say that no one has done a better job than Bobby Brantley.

Now there are times when, I'm sure, if brains were leather, Bobby couldn't saddle a June bug. But when it comes to protecting me, he's a redneck Hercules. Bobby is one of those big, homegrown country boys who's tough enough to chew up a ten-penny nail and spit out a barbed-wire fence. We've been in some pretty hairy situations together—many of them with some of the biggest, burliest men you've ever seen. Through it all, I've never seen Bobby taken out by anyone. When we leave for a repo, no matter what the odds, Bobby always makes sure we lick the situation. I've seen him stand toe-to-toe with giants and smile as he tells 'em it's not that he doesn't care what they have to say, he just feels they're too insignificant to listen to.

Bobby hasn't been with my company too long (maybe about as long as him and his third wife have been together, and that's about eight months). But in that time I've seen him grab more than one tiger by the tail and fight him off with a switch in the dark for me. But Bobby has two small downfalls. The first is that he's never wrong. Things are always going to be his way or the highway. But in his case, I'd have to admit he's well worth the hassle. I've worked with too many guys who were all hat and no cattle. Although nine times out of ten, doing a repo with Bobby is about as much fun as a nosebleed, he's gotten pretty proficient at getting me out unhurt.

Bobby's second downfall is his complete lack of people skills. Bobby thinks that he meets all people by destiny, and those he meets during a repo were sent to him as punishment. Whenever we get out of our truck to grab a vehicle and find ourselves having to interact with people, Bobby immediately has the attitude that he was having a great day and they shouldn't screw it up by talking. So I decided that anytime we head out to do a repo and I'm pretty sure it's gonna be an easy run, I'll let Bobby take the lead and work on his people skills.

Every time I tell Bobby I'm going to let him take the lead, he looks about as happy as a dead possum on the Interstate. He's always telling me that his job is to have my back; if I decide to slap the bull, he's going to dog him. I've been trying to teach Bobby that the art of repossession is a mental chess game, and we can win as many battles with a slick tongue as we can with force. But Bobby thinks he's so bad he can make a man put back stuff he hasn't even stolen yet, so it's hard to win him over to my point of view. Yet I know the snail made it to the Ark through perseverance, so I keep trying to convince Bobby every chance I get.

One day I got a call from one of our lien holders. They needed to repossess a car from an older lady who lived by herself in a trailer park. The manager asked me to be exceptionally nice, 'cause he had a soft place in his heart for this lady. He really didn't want to repossess her car, but he couldn't get her to communicate with him. He did tell me she was a sweet old lady, but she had enough mouth for five sets of teeth.

Well, I figured that I really didn't have a dog in this fight and it would be the perfect chance to let Bobby work on his verbal persuasion. When I explained the situation to Bobby, he seemed as excited as a legless frog at an all-night IHOP. I told him that I would run point and take the spotter car; he could drive the tow truck and do the hooking and talking. Since this was a single older lady, he should be able to talk her right out of her keys. Try as I might, I just couldn't get him sold on the idea. "Ronnie," he said, "I'd rather have a broke back in hell than have to deal with someone on a repossession. That's not my cup of tea."

I knew Bobby would eventually come around to seeing things my way; I just had to do some serious persuading. Finally, we headed out to the little old lady's trailer, and I just knew this would be an easy repo and a great chance for Bobby to sharpen his people skills. As soon as we turned the bend into the trailer park, we spotted a white Sunfire parked at the address. I jumped out and checked the VIN on it to make sure it was the right car. After verifying it, I motioned to Bobby (who was sitting in the tow truck) to come on out to hook and strap the car. I would go knock on the door to see if anyone was home.

Bobby backed up the tow truck and lifted the car while I strapped the far side. As Bobby got out to strap his side, I went to the door to see if we could get the lady outside so Bobby could talk her out of the keys. Well, as soon as she opened the door, I knew from the look on her face that she was hotter than a two-dollar pistol. I didn't have to say a word—she knew why we were there. The only question she had was, "Who's in charge of this situation?"

I stopped for all of two seconds before I pointed to Bobby and said, "That's the owner right there, ma'am. His name is Bobby Brantley." About that time, Bobby turned around and looked like a deer caught in headlights by a hand grenade. He could see this little old lady didn't need a car to drive: she needed a broom to ride! But I guess that broom was broken, 'cause she came out of the trailer with a regular ol' kitchen broom—and the intention of taking out what she saw as the trash.

Bobby immediately started talking politely, trying to explain to her that we were just doing our job and he was sorry.

She looked him over and said, "I'm sorry too."

"What are you sorry for?"

"This!"

Faster than you can lick a fried chocolate skillet, she lit into him with that broom like a pack of piranhas on a chicken leg. There's big Bobby running from the Wicked Witch of the East around the tow truck while she's sweeping him off his feet. The entire time, he's yelling, "Ronnie! Ronnie, help me!"

I yelled out, "Ma'am, listen, please!"

She stopped dead in her tracks and spun around to look at me. It was at that point I knew I was going to be as much use to Bobby as a prefabricated post-hole digger. "You want some of this too, Mr. Sonic the Hedgehog?" she barked, referring to my hairstyle.

I looked at her and said, "No, ma'am. I would rather be chained to the underbelly of a moose during mating season than to deal with you."

Then I bid her a fond farewell and, as I was jumping in my spotter car, saw she had turned her attention—and that broom—back to Bobby. I put the truck in reverse and heard Bobby yelling, "Ronnie! Where do you think you're going?"

"Hey, Bo," I answered just as she broke that broom over his head, "looks like you got this one under control!" And he went to running like a fat man chasing a doughnut downhill.

I headed back to the shop, content to let him work on his people skills. A few minutes later he called and told me he finally got out of there after she wore herself out beating him with that broom.

I got all the employees to go outside and sweep the parking lot as Bobby pulled up, and that made him madder than a pack of rabid wolves on a three-legged rabbit. He jumped out of the truck and just glared at me.

"Hey, Bo, looks like she swept you off your feet!"

He tossed me the keys and said, "Right. Funny, man. I'm done for the day. I've had enough of you—and this place."

I said, "Well, at least tell me: Did you learn anything during this incident?"

"I sure did," Bobby replied. "I learned I used to have a handle on life—but now it's broken." Then he drove off into the sunset.

[Other Sayin's]

1. I hate his stomach for holding his guts.
2. I could eat the tail end out of a ragdoll.
3. I ain't got no dog in that fight.
4. Call me butter 'cause I'm on a roll.
5. That dog won't hunt.
6. Now, that's how you tree a blind possum.
7. He had no idea whose weeds he just pissed in.
8. I used to be schizophrenic . . . but now we're all OK.
9. Hell and half of Georgia.
10. Now, that's just how a cow eats cabbage.
11. High-stepping like a rooster in deep mud.
12. Up and down like whores' drawers.
13. Ain't no thing but a chicken wing.
14. Screaming like a mashed cat.
15. Bo, the only place you'll find sympathy around here is between "symbol" and "syphilis" in the dictionary.
16. Latched on like a big-nosed mosquito at a blood bank.
17. I skinned that like a Georgia catfish.

Final Thoughts
from an Uncommon Mind

Two years before I began writing this book, I had reached the end of my rope. The thread was frayed and my grip was slipping fast. Then I opened an old, worn-out book that had been lying around my house for years. As I read the pages, one after another, I could not stop the flood of tears that emptied from my soul. The chaotic life I had been living seemed aimless, and the turmoil that I had learned to accept as normal flooded out of my body. I wept tears of blood into a pool of salvation and hit my knees with a determination to find the source.

It was in that moment that I met God for the second time in my life—having run from Him when I was eighteen. I saw a pasture and I was standing at its gate. Down the hill was a house with soothing lights that seemed to pull me toward them. It was as if a celebratory festival was in progress, and I could sense the joy and peace that abounded below. I believed I would never be welcome in such a place, for I was a worthless thief and a killer of man.

Then He spoke. It seemed as if the mountains themselves were shaken from their foundations. "Do not be afraid, for I have been expecting you. Come, for I know you are thirsty, and I have water. Sit, for I know you are hungry, and I have much for you to feed upon."

I looked at my feet and saw I was chained to the ground

with shackles of self-pity. The chains were heavy, and each time I tried to free myself from them, they tightened around my ankles. I looked around and saw wolves, circling and growling. Scraps of meat hung from their bloodthirsty jaws, and their razor-edged teeth seemed to glimmer in the moonlight. Each time I pulled to free myself, I became more entangled in the past: my worthlessness, my addictions, the harm I had caused this world, the hearts I had broken, the people I had ruined. I felt myself being pulled back toward the woods and the darkness where those just like me were calling my name.

I looked back one last time toward the house and saw the man, arms still open. He spoke again: "Come home, son. It's time for you to come home."

I finally replied, "But sir, I am worthless. I have wasted my talents. I have thrown my life to the wolves. I have lied, stolen, envied, falsely accused my friends. Sir, I have done things from which I cannot return. I have lived in the darkness so long I can no longer see the light. I have wallowed in sin and it exudes from every pore of my existence. I have danced with the devil and drunk from his cup of damnation."

There was a long silence. Time seemed to stand still. I watched the man, but it appeared he was getting farther away; the light was fading and night was again upon me. A cold chill crept through me. I felt alone and desolate.

It was at that moment that a light brighter than anything I had ever seen appeared. It blinded me, so I had to cover my face, but its warmth was indescribable and the peace that dwelled within it was unquestionable. Then a loud voice bellowed from the house: "I DO NOT CARE WHAT YOU HAVE DONE. I DO NOT CARE WHAT YOU

HAVE BECOME. JUST COME HOME, BECAUSE I STILL
LOVE YOU."

As I raised a hand over my eyes to see where the voice
was coming from, I saw an object hurtling toward me. I
reached into the air to catch it, and as I brought it down
and opened my hand, I saw it was a key.

Then He said, "You, in the hills, release my child, for he
is coming home."

I reached down toward the chains that had held me for
so long, and as soon as I put the key in the lock, the chains
exploded off my ankles. The weight of the world fell from
me, and I realized I was free.

I turned and ran toward the pasture, blew through the
gate, and sprinted as fast as my legs would move toward
the house. I could hear the deafening screams behind me,
urging me to turn around and come back, trying to fill my
mind with thoughts that I was not worthy to cross the pasture. I ran into the man's arms, speechless, with tears ca-
reening down my cheeks.

He simply said, "Welcome home, son. Welcome home."

He stepped in front of me and raised His hands toward
heaven, and I could see blood flowing from them. I fell to
my knees and saw blood flowing from His feet. He said,
"This is my child, and his name is forever written in the
Lamb's Book of Life. His sins have been paid for by the
blood that flows from my body. He is now and forever
sealed and a son in my Father's house."

He held up His hands again and said, "Father, your son
has come home. The one sheep was again found, and
snatched from the mouths of the wolves. He is scarred and
battered, but he is home and now he is whole."

As I looked up I saw my wife by my side praying, tears

streaming down her face. My children were speechless, and there was a glow emanating from each of them. My wife looked at me and said, "Ronnie, we are finally all gonna go home together."

Most prolific moments are just that: a moment. Not mine. My prolific moment has taken thirty-four years to develop. When my moment happened, I wasn't standing in the line of life suddenly having an epiphany; thoughts did not just pass through my mind aimlessly, sparking a wonder of revelation in a second of discovery. I have had to fight for every foot of my existence; I have bled for every minute of every vision I've had; I have shed a dry tear for every failure, and I couldn't begin to describe the bittersweet smell of understanding in my life.

My battlefield has always been in my own mind, with victory at neither end. My life is lived for the existence of others: those to whom I owe everything but whom I always seem to disappoint. I cannot change what I have lived; I cannot return to the battlefield of yesterday and alter the fight. I must stand upon the foundation I have laid, held together for the most part by those who surround me—for the cracks are great and the stability is attacked daily by the harsh waters of time and memory.

So I struggle on the battlefield, tired and sore from raging poundings, broken and limp from the relentless beatings. But I struggle still. I never surrender, never stop, never succumb—and never, ever walk away.

This field is where I will live out my days that the sword has sharpened with knowledge, the body has protected with will, and my eyes have adorned with fire and an unquenchable burn. The fire burns through every pore of my body, the flame keeps us aglow and forces that next step.

If only the sword had been sharper when I began this quest; if only the map had more detail and the path had been more vividly lit; or if I had a guide to lead me around the obstacles instead of falling hopelessly into each one. Of course, if I had these things, I would not be myself. I chose this path. I took each step—some with careful thought, others with a blinding speed, my eyes wide shut. But each step belongs to me and to no one else.

So the battle is mine. I cannot control the war, but I can hold the field, relentlessly stand firm, and protect the borders. Fear is now my ally. I have learned to twist it into hope.

I will fight on until my body decays and my breath is stolen. At that time I pray my battle will have been successful and that those for whom I fought will have to fight no more. They may have found it a horror to live by my side, but I found it an honor to die by theirs. Their fields will be covered in flowers of concrete so that they will never wilt but will, instead, reap a harvest of protection for those wandering soldiers who have lost their will to fight, their ability to lead, or their grasp on truth.

This is my epiphany, and the years of battle my prolific moment. And though it will never be defining, it will also never be relinquished.

So now, two years later, I help run the eastern chapter of Dirt Church. We stop into fields, homes, and workplaces to preach the Gospel and bring one sheep at a time back across that pasture. We go into the hills, with the protection of our God, and snatch victory from the well-clamped claws of the enemy's grip. And this is our message:

NO MATTER WHAT YOU HAVE DONE, NO MAT-
TER WHAT YOU HAVE BECOME, YOU CAN COME
HOME.

God made dirt . . . and dirt should not hurt. Live the
message and preach the blessings.
—*Lizard Lick Dirt Church and Revelation Ron*

[One Last Word]

1. Backstroke it all the way to the front door.

2. That makes as much sense as taking a duck to a chicken fight.

3. Just shove an umbrella up his butt and call it a hurricane.

4. I've known him since dirt was clean.

5. Bo, you gotta be quieter than a mouse peeing on cotton.

6. I'm as tired as a four-armed tobacco picker on a hot day looking for a glass of ice water.

7. That'll go over like a pregnant pole-vaulter.

8. That'll go over like socks on a porcupine.

9. That runs off me like water off a duck's back.

10. That makes about as much sense as doing an oil change on a wrecked car.

11. You'd better put on some boots and pack a lunch, 'cause it's gonna be an all-day, uphill thing.

12. Getting on this train is a whole lot easier than getting off.

13. I gave you heaven and earth and you still want a tobacco field in hell?

14. Bo, I'm happy. Don't screw it up by talking.

15. Don't buy nothing that has a handle. That could mean work.

16. It's so dry, the river only runs twice a week.

17. I can squeeze a quarter so tight, Washington will say uncle.

Acknowledgments

God put us here, fans keep us here. Above all else I wanna thank my Savior and Redeemer Jesus Christ for granting me the courage to live this life, the fortitude to endure its trials, the encouragement to weather the tribulations, and the *love* he shows by accepting me as his child even when I don't acknowledge him as my father.

To a true human angel, my mother, for never giving up on me and for teaching me that love isn't love until you give it away. You always tried to protect me, usually from myself, but you never wavered in your belief in me, and I am forever indebted to you for all the years you spent fighting on your knees for my salvation and sanity. Without you, the only work I would have ever published would have been my epitaph. Momma, I never knew where I was going, but I always knew I was welcome to come Home To.

Pops, for just being Pops and never giving a darn. Life was always an adventure because of you, and I hope I grow to be the dad you are.

To my brother, Jason. Even though we view life through different lenses, we have walked many a mile side by side, and you'll always be my brother. This book reflects your journey, too.

To my little sister, Sandy, for your willingness to stand alone when you thought you were right, and to stand up for yourself—especially to me—lighting a new path on which to walk.

To my Amy, you have endured many years of harsh storms for small bouts of sunshine with me. The path has been rocky, and I know at times the chaos seemed endless. The foundation we built our lives on is filled with cracks because of my stubbornness and pride. But you never left my side, and many times you held me up when my knees were too weak to stand, and you stood in front of me when my mind was too weak to fight. You are what I thank God for every day above all else. You are the perfect inspiration for this book, and your love has allowed me to write these tales. The foundation is cracked, the building is aged, the yard is overgrown, but the love that abides in this house overflows from every corner. You will always be my Lil Firecracker.

To my beautiful daughter Alexa, you are why I love the rain, and though we never see eye to eye and I will always be that uncool, out-of-touch dad, I will gladly trade my life for yours any day. You are my firstborn, my proudest achievement, and my greatest success. You will always be Lexi Lou, and you will always be Daddy's little girl.

To my Cowboy Alex, you inspire me to want to be a better dad, a kinder person, a gentler father, and a best friend every day. I wrote these stories wondering what tales you will have to tell me in the years to come, and I stand in awe of your faith and your magic, both in your hands and in your heart. Gooder men there may be, greater men there will never be than you.

To chunky monkey, my lil' Gabey Baby, you're my running back, and when you're not cutting through defensive lines, you're scoring touchdowns with everyone you meet. If people in this world had one-tenth of your attitude, determination, and love, there would never be a war fought or a heart broke. You truly inspire me, son, and it will always be Team Shirley.

To Maggie Mae Manhattan, you're the culmination of a lifetime of mistakes and decades of wrong turns, and living proof that perfection can come from such things. I don't know what I did to deserve such a princess, but your name carries such meaning and your smile carries light into the darkest night. You are an inspiration to the uninspired and proof that the path we choose does make all the difference.

To my grandma Myrtie Harris, who taught me how to fish and fight but also showed me how to love. I will be seeing you soon. Hold the gates open.

To Brian King: Friends come and go, but brothers always stick together—till the end, Kingpin.

To Bobby Brantley, for walking this road with me, even in the harsh storms. Thanks for not running for shelter.

To Johnny Perry: You had the greatest grip in the world but couldn't hold back the hands of destiny; but in your death, you gave me new life. I have been able to accomplish all this because of you.

To Brooks Ray: Thanks for just being "Bubba" to me.

To my crew at Lizard Lick Towing and Recovery: Brian, Patty, Steve, Bumpy, Brandon, Ricky, for busting your tails so we could make this happen, and for putting up with me in crunch time. You are the reason we have gotten to where we are and the reason we are a success in this field.

To each and every one of my lien holders, for having the faith not only to add me, but to keep me as part of their collection arsenal.

To the repossession industry, for letting me prove myself in such a competitive field and make "You have been licked" the reason debtors hate us, lien holders love us, and repo agents all over the world want to be just like us.

To truTV for taking the chance on us and allowing us to Lick the entire world. This book is a product of your support.

To my newfound brother DeeJay Silver—Holler and Hair Products.

Thank you to Mark Schlabach and Nena Medonia for making this book a reality. I appreciate your hard work and dedication.

Thanks to my manager, Mrs. Carri at NVRDUL, who is tougher than Tarzan feet, quicker than a cheetah on Amtrak, slicker than snot and mashed bananas, and the greatest rattlesnake killer to ever come outta the state of Texas. This book would have never found daylight without your help.

And to everyone else who has played any part in my life, I thank you.